A MOTHER'S LETTERS

Concepción Cabrera de Armida (Conchita)

A Mother's Letters

A Vision of Faith in Everyday Life

Compiled and annotated by
SISTER DOLORES ICAZA CONREY, R.C.S.C.J.

Translated by MARY McCANDLESS

ST PAULS

Originally published in Spanish under the title *Cartas de una madre de familia — Concepción Cabrera de Armida* by Ediciones Cimiento, A.C. © R.C.S.C.J., Mexico D.F., 1986

Library of Congress Cataloging-in-Publication Data

Conchita, 1862-1937.
   [Cartas de una madre de familia. English]
   A mother's letters / Concepcion Cabrera de Armida (Conchita);
compiled and annotated by Dolores Icaza Conrey.
      p. cm.
   Includes bibliographical references.
   ISBN 0-8189-0961-7
   1. Conchita, 1862-1937—Correspondence. 2.
Catholics—Mexico—Correspondence. 3. Spiritual life—Catholic Church.
I. Icaza Conrey, Dolores. II. Title.

   BX4705.C742A4 2004
   282'.092—dc22
                            2003022240

Nihil Obstat:
R.P. Pablo Vera Olvera, M.Sp.S.
Censor.

Imprimatur:
Monsignor Francisco Lomelí L., Auxiliary Archbishop of México
México City, January 28, 1986

Imprimi Potest:
R.M. Ma. Guadalupe Labarthe, Sup. Gral. R.C.S.C.J.

The Nihil Obstat and Imprimatur are official declarations
that a book or pamphlet is free of doctrinal or moral
error. No implication is contained therein that those
who have granted the Nihil Obstat and Imprimatur agree
with the contents, opinions or statements expressed.

First printing in Spanish: 1986
Second printing in Spanish: 1991
First printing in Italian: 1988

Produced and designed in the United States of America by the
Fathers and Brothers of the Society of St. Paul,
2187 Victory Boulevard, Staten Island, New York 10314-6603,
as part of their communications apostolate.

ISBN: 0-8189-0961-7

Printing Information:

Current Printing - first digit   2 3 4 5 6 7 8 9 10

Year of Current Printing - first year shown

      2014 2015 2016 2017 2018 2019 2020 2021 2022

Dedication

To the Immaculate Heart of Mary

Concepción Cabrera de Armida with her children in 1904:
(standing from the left) Salvador, Concepción, Francisco,
Manuel, (sitting from the left) Pablo, Guadalupe, Ignacio

Table of Contents

To Her Brothers and Sisters In-Law on the Armida Side

To Her Grandchildren

To Her Nephews and Nieces, Cabrera Family

To Her In-Laws: Nieces and Nephews, Armida Family

Presentation

I thank God from Whom all goodness comes and am pleased to present these carefully selected letters of the Venerable Servant of God, Concepción Cabrera de Armida to her children, brothers and sisters, nieces and nephews, etc., compiled and annotated with reverent love and exacting competence by Sister María Dolores Icaza Conrey.

Sister Dolores finished her studies in Arts and Letters at the Autonomous University of Mexico. She majored in Sacred Scriptures at the Biblical Institute of the Missionaries of the Holy Spirit, at the "Altillo" in Coyoacán. She has published two books: *Let Us Live the Psalms*, and *A Commentary on the Lord's Prayer and the Hail Mary*. For many years, she has collaborated in the enormous task of ordering and transcribing the writings of the Venerable Servant of God, Concepción Cabrera de Armida. She also assisted the well-known author Michel Marie Philipon, O.P., Th.D., on his book entitled, in the original French, *Journal Spirituel d'une mère de Famille*. It is available in English as *Conchita: A Mother's Spiritual Diary* (Alba House, 1978).

I believe that this sampling of Concepción Cabrera de Armida's letters will make known this Venerable Servant of God in her identity as a Mother totally immersed in her world as a lay person dedicated to the work of salvation in Jesus, Priest and Victim.

Ma. Guadalupe Labarthe, R.C.S.C.J.
Superior General

Prologue

Concepción Cabrera de Armida — in her life and her works — constitutes a noteworthy religious phenomenon in twentieth century Mexico. She was the inspiration for the Congregation of the Sisters of the Cross of the Sacred Heart of Jesus, a contemplative religious congregation in whose bosom she died, having received special permission to pronounce religious vows valid at the moment of her death; for the Congregation of the Missionaries of the Holy Spirit together with Father Félix de Jesús Rougier, and for other works jointly called "of the Cross"; she inspired a spirituality flowing from her personal experience in a life of continuous and intimate relationship with the Lord. The overflowing richness of her spiritual life compelled her to write — by the order of her spiritual director — pages and pages that reveal spiritual and mystical experiences that would astound the world when they became known, according to the testimony of the well-known Dominican theologian Michel M. Philipon, O.P., who came to Mexico expressly to study her life and her works. He published his book and died in Mexico while occupied with this task.

One might think that such a person would have had religious life as her vocation and that she would have spent her days in the retirement of a convent, in the intimacy of contemplation, and in the enterprises and responsibilities of her apostolate. But it was not so. Concepción Cabrera de Armida was a woman living in the world, a wife and a mother. She took part in the culture and society of her time. She loved her husband Francisco Armida with whom she had nine children whom they raised and educated. After seventeen years of marriage she became a widow. One can affirm that it was precisely from this experience of married life, of her spousal union, of her motherhood, that the Lord called her to a profound spiritual experience.

This is precisely what renders her life and her work so unique. This is what makes this book so interesting.

During her life, Concepción Cabrera de Armida wrote numerous letters to her mother, brothers and sisters, to her husband and children, and other relatives. Sister Dolores Icaza, Sister of the Cross, who aided Father Philipon in his work, offers in this book a selection of Conchita's letters to her relatives. Sister Dolores adds brief notes that explain to the readers something about the persons to whom they are addressed, and the circumstances in which they were written. A selection made with love and care is possible only when one has a deep knowledge of the person who wrote these letters.

These letters reveal, in the course of everyday incidents as well as in the great events of life, a vision of faith, and an abundance of supernatural life that manifests itself and grows as a counterpoint to daily experiences. This vision penetrates everything, the intimate exchanges, the affectionate bond with members of her own family whom she loved up to the end, the difficulties in personal relationships, the joys and sorrows, the birth and the death of her loved ones, health and sickness, good and bad fortune and even the exchange of kitchen recipes and homemade remedies.

Mrs. Armida lived in the world. That is to say she lived in the culture and events of her time — the final third of the nineteenth century and the first part of the twentieth. In this sense, she was a typical Mexican Christian wife and mother, of whom we have known many in various social positions. Her world was that of a traditional Catholic family of good economic standing, and her life unfolded between her native province, San Luis Potosí, and Mexico City. She would have liked to see Mexico an officially Catholic country, from the President on down. What she actually lived was the separation of Church and State, the religious persecution of the twenties, the closing of Catholic schools, and the socialist education that took place in the following decade.

One notices the traditional Catholic attitude of mistrust of the Mexican governments which she judges to be led by Freemasonry and Communism. Though today things have changed culturally, her view of marital relationships and the role of a woman in marriage were also traditional. Cultural values change, but in them permanent human values shine forth, especially the values of faith and the supernatural life.

The way in which her constant and intimate relationship with God gave her a serene wisdom when applied to human affairs, enabling her to penetrate hearts and to know and understand problems is highly remarkable. This is a gift of the Holy Spirit and cannot be learned. Her letters are filled with examples. Her central theme is love, the primacy of love. In some of her most beautiful and touching letters she speaks at length about her experience of love. She is, as she says herself, enamored of love itself. Not, certainly as a sentimental teen-age emotion which is not yet firmly directed, but rather in her personal love experience with Him Who is Love Itself, Christ. She writes: "My fiery heart flings itself with passion to love Him Who is Love Itself." Can we not find here the starting point of her spirituality of the Cross? "Worldly loves are supernaturalized with sacrifice," she says. Sacrifice, totally free action. An act of love. Not a sentiment based on guilt or self-destruction. Not an act of alienation, but an oblation or self-denial for love's sake. This is the

Cross. Therefore not a rejection nor a flight from the world — not even into the bosom of a contemplative community that organizes life outside the ways of the world — but rather a service to the world in loving solidarity with one's neighbor, sometimes not understood easily by simple human logic.

One may go through the pages of these letters with the certainty of finding a real skill in perception that is very revealing. Let us present some examples:

On peace as a condition for communal life, as a means that makes possible the flourishing of love, and the important role a woman has in obtaining it and conserving it: "Peace, peace, no matter what the cost." This is how she sees a family. This is how she tried to make her own family.

"The heart of Jesus is profoundly maternal... God is three times a Saint and a thousand times a Mother."

"Judas' disgrace was not his treachery, but not having believed in Jesus' love, which is God's forgiveness."

Mrs. Armida had a great appreciation and a deep insight regarding religious life. When she experienced the nearness of her death, she wrote about her longing to die as a Sister of the Cross, with a religious habit and vows. The Lord granted her desires. Her most beautiful letters are those written to her two religious children: Manuel, a Jesuit priest and religious, and Concepción — as herself — who received the name of Teresa de María Inmaculada. She must have written many letters to bishops and priests, brothers and sisters.

I can affirm that her experience of human love in all its dimensions, her primary vocation as spouse and mother and her widowhood, allowed her to penetrate the depths of religious life with a particular vision. Not that this experience was strictly necessary to this end. Indeed, it is the exception. But this was exactly the reality that God allowed her to live and it permeates all of her works and is noticeable in the letters to her relatives. To make this evident is one of the merits of this selection of letters, which, on being published, will contribute to the knowledge and comprehension of the life and works of Concepción Cabrera de Armida: wife, mother, and religious inspiration.

Easter, 1982
Raúl Medina Mora

Note: Raúl Medina Mora y Martín del Campo, Attorney at Law, was born into a profoundly Catholic family. He married Luisa Icaza Conrey on June 2, 1949. Their marriage was blessed by Father Julio J. Vértiz, S.J., spiritual director to both of them. They are the parents of nine children. Raúl was for twelve years the private secretary to Antonio Bermúdez of Petróleos Mexicanos. Afterwards, he established his own Law Office. He and his wife collaborated generously in the Mexican Institute of Political Studies and in the Christian Family Movement — first with Engineer José Alvarez Icaza and his wife Luz Longoria, and later, when the latter took charge of the Movement in all of Latin America, Raúl and Luisa took charge of it in Mexico. For this reason they have had frequent contacts with the Mexican bishops, priests and varied social and religious sectors in whose service they have employed their human and cultural talents.

Introduction

This selection of the letters of Concepción Cabrera de Armida to her relatives is the result of several years of secluded and devoted reading and study of this portion of the literary output of the Venerable Servant of God.

It seems to us that in these letters one may better appreciate the human aspect of this great Mexican woman: her rich personality as daughter, spouse, mother, sister, aunt, godmother, and friend. We may find in them her affective, realistic, practical, psychological, religious, humorous and artistic gifts. Through her simplicity, the everyday life of this mother — like any of our own mothers — blossoms forth, enhanced by the impact that her intense spiritual life confers. The warmth that the love of God communicates to her sets her on fire, and grants her light and power that makes her very close to us and allows us to see small, everyday things with the splendor derived from the profound purpose of every human happening: its divine origin and its equally supernatural goal.

All of this without succumbing to annoying pedagogy: she teaches through her living, and speaks through her loving. The sincere and generous tenderness that makes her vitally interested in her loved ones, appearing very close to them in every circumstance with a loyal and sincere affection, always eager to share their sufferings and joys, bringing relief to the former and increase to the latter, is evident in her written correspondence.

In this volume, we present only a sample of her correspondence with her relatives. Possibly, in the near future, other selections of the letters of our Potosinean mystic may appear and perhaps even a critical edition of her whole epistolary work.

In the Archive of the Sisters of the Cross of the Sacred Heart of Jesus — from where we have taken our material — are kept 25 volumes of the letters, a copy of the ones sent to Rome for the Cause of Beatification. Among them:

4 volumes are addressed to her relatives, with 447 letters
1 volume to Mexican bishops, with 59 letters
3 volumes to Archbishop Luis M. Martínez, with 246 letters
7 volumes to Archbishop Leopoldo Ruíz y Flores, with 597 letters
1 volume to different Priests, with 248 letters
3 volumes to Father Félix de Jesús Rougier, with 344 letters
1 volume to several Missionaries of the Holy Spirit, with 167 letters
1 volume to Father Thomas Fallon, M.Sp.S., with 33 letters
1 volume to Father Edmundo Iturbide, M.Sp.S., with 100 letters
1 volume to Fr. José Guadalupe Treviño, M.Sp.S., with 219 letters
3 volumes to different Sisters of the Cross, with 350 letters

In making the selection, we attempted to include a representative sample of correspondents and themes. When ordering the letters, we preferred to order them according to the correspondents, so as to facilitate the perception of the characteristic relationship between Mrs. Armida and her relatives. But when arranging the letters of each person, we did follow a chronological order, so that the natural progression of each relationship would be more evident.

It was my intention to offer these letters in their original simplicity without hiding or adding anything, so that she would present herself to us as she was in her daily life as a woman, spouse, and Mexican mother at the end of the 19th and beginning of the 20th century, with all the richness and poverty of this history so full of political, religious, and social events.

So that our contact with her would be more real, I preserved the familiar simplicity of her writings. Preceding every letter, I placed a brief note about the person to whom she was writing and that person's relationship with Mrs. Armida. As the work advanced, I found it useful to add a few notes to explain a Mexican idiom or a familiar expression, or some data that would facilitate the understanding of a vital situation referred to in a letter. I added, as far as it was possible, some references to people and places referred to in the writing, so as to aid people who might be strangers to the family background of the Venerable Servant of God.

With the kind authorization of Father Luis Ruíz Vázquez, M.Sp.S., we included a brief biography of Mrs. Armida at the beginning of the volume. My brother-in-law, Raúl Medina Mora, Attorney at Law, had the kindness to write a prologue for this collection of letters. Having been President of the Christian Family Movement along with my sister Luisa, and for having been the parent of nine children, just like Mr. and Mrs. Armida, he was considered to be an appropriate person from the literary, social, cultural, and religious point of view.

At the end, we included a bibliography so as to facilitate further information for anyone wishing it after the reading of these letters. There is also a chronology of the life of Mrs. Armida to make it possible to locate each letter in the context of her life, as well as a brief note about her spiritual directors.

Biographical Synthesis

The Venerable Concepción Cabrera de Armida (Conchita) lived all of the states of life possible for a Christian woman: she was a single young lady, a spouse, the mother of nine children, widow, and a religious by desire, although not within the actualized frame of religious life.

She was born in Mexico in the city of San Luis Potosí, on December 8, 1862. In baptism she received the name of María de la Concepción. She was a feeble baby and she had to be taken to the country to reinforce her health.

She was happy and playful like all children: her naivety was noticeable and was reflected in her eyes up to her old age.

An elegant and beautiful young lady, she attended balls, theaters, society reunions, and family parties. She had many suitors but she only loved one of them: Francisco Armida.

There were no religious orders in her native land, and so she knew no other vocation than marriage. She loved her husband as pure souls do, intensely and with a love that, far from distancing her from God's love, instead founded in her heart a single unique love.

She was married at twenty-two. During the seventeen years of her marriage, she had nine children. She liked to play the piano, to sing, and to go horseback riding.

Conchita lived twenty-two years single, seventeen married, and thirty-six widowed. By an indult given by Pope Saint Pius X, she died belonging spiritually to the Congregation of the Sisters of the Cross of the Sacred Heart of Jesus, inspired by her.

From her youth, she had a deep desire for perfection, but no one taught her the way. During 1893, the Lord provided her with a wise spiritual director who taught her the way of perfection. Purity of heart, the spirit of sacrifice, humility, and a great knowledge of God, in spite of her receiving only basic instruction, were outstanding in her life.

The Mystery of Jesus Crucified attracted Conchita. Her fidelity to this attraction led her to deepen her knowledge of the mystery of Jesus' sacrifice, the supreme act of His priesthood. Jesus Priest, Jesus Victim, Jesus Altar are the three complementary aspects of the priesthood of which Conchita reminds the Church today.

After many spiritual purifications she received the grace of a particular kind of spiritual fruitfulness which she herself called a "mystical incarnation." This was her principal grace which she received on March 25, 1906, when she was forty-four.

Conchita was instrumental in inspiring in the Church the five Works of the Cross: (1) the Apostleship of the Cross, (2) the Covenant of Love with the Sacred Heart of Jesus, both of these for laity, (3) the Fraternity of Christ Priest, for priests and bishops who desire to live the spirituality of the Cross and to work in spreading this devotion, (4) the Sisters of the Cross of the Sacred Heart of Jesus, a contemplative Congregation of Religious, and (5) the Missionaries of the Holy Spirit, who are priests and brothers.

After over a century of existence and on verification of the fruits they have borne, one can affirm that these Works, indeed, come from God.

Characteristic of all these Works is the spirituality of the Cross, a devotion manifested in the numerous writings of Conchita and lived by her in its utmost perfection, as a model for all souls drawn to the Cross. These Works are inspired by a deep priestly and Trinitarian spirit, and aim to diffuse in all the Church the Kingdom of the Holy Spirit, which is the reign of the love and of the Cross of our Savior.

The Venerable Servant of God died on March 3, 1937, leaving behind her in all the places and among all the people she touched, especially priests and bishops, her reputation for holiness.

The Curia of the Archdiocese of Mexico City initiated a study of her reputation for holiness on April 13, 1957 (Ordinary Process), and two others on May 29, 1958, one de non cultu (or absence of cult) to prove that the decrees regarding the prohibition of public worship of servants before their beatification had been obeyed, and the other of her writings. On February 24, 1959, the first part of this second Process was concluded, and on May 30 the Process regarding her reputation for holiness was completed. On October 27, 1959, the study of her writings was finished.

On September 29, 1959, the results of these three procedures were taken to Rome and her cause for canonization was canonically opened with a decree of the Congregation for the Causes of the Saints.

At present this process is well under way.

Luis Ruiz Vázquez, M.Sp.S.

Note: Her writings were examined over a period of sixteen years and on February 15, 1974, a favorable response was received. Then the Processes that took place in Mexico were examined to see if they were able to demonstrate that her life had been thoroughly wholesome and worthy to be proposed as a model and if her reputation for holiness was authentic and based upon a truly heroic practice of the virtues. The Congregation for the Causes of the Saints gave its favorable opinion.

On May 11, 1982, the cause of Mrs. Armida was approved by the Pope, who gave orders to Cardinal Ernesto Corripio Ahumada to begin a new process to clarify exhaustively the questions posed by the Promoter of the Faith. This process was initiated on July 20, 1982 and was called "Apostolic" because it was undertaken through the initiative of the Holy Father. It was concluded on September 8, 1984.

Before informing the Holy Father of the results, a cardinal relator examined, studied, summarized, ordered, and clarified everything. His conclusions were given to the Congregation for the Saints on July 23, 1992.

Once all these requirements were met, the Holy Father confirmed the results declaring Concepción Cabrera de Armida "Venerable": The theological virtues of Faith, Hope and Love toward both God and neighbor, as well as the cardinal virtues of Prudence, Justice, Temperance and Fortitude and those virtues related to them, are clearly acknowledged to have been practiced in a heroic degree by the Venerable Servant of God Concepción Cabrera de Armida, widow and mother of nine children.

He ordered this decree to be officially promulgated and entered into the Acts of the Congregation for the Causes of the Saints on December 22, 1999.

Beatification and canonization depend principally on Our Lord, because miracles must take place, and they are the "signature of God." One miracle has already been submitted for study on September 28, 1992.

After each letter we shall place its reference: *L.R., Vol. I/7 (Letters to her Relatives, Volume I, letter 7).*

LETTERS TO HER RELATIVES
4 Volumes

Name and Relationship	Chosen Letters	Number in Existence	Order
Clara Arias de Cabrera (mother)	1	1	1
Francisco, Salvador, Lupe (children)	1	1	2
Francisco Armida Cabrera (eldest son)	1	5	3
Elisa Baz (daughter-in-law)	1	1	3a
Manuel Armida Cabrera (son-priest)	21	58	4-24
Concha Armida Cabrera (daughter-religious)	12	222	25-36
Ignacio Armida Cabrera (married son)	6	10	37-42
Chabela Morán (daughter-in-law)	6	10	43-48
Salvador Armida Cabrera (married son)	4	25	49-52
Amada Gutiérrez (daughter-in-law)	3	5	53-55
Guadalupe Armida Cabrera (married daughter)	2	11	56-57
Carlota Wilson (sister-in-law)	2	2	58-59
Fr. Primitivo Cabrera (brother-priest)	1	4	60
Francisco Cabrera Arias (brother)	4	12	61-64
Rosario Armida de V. (sister-in-law)	2	6	65-66
Antonio Armida & Emilia (brother & sister-in-law)	4	10	67-70
Manuel Armida Morán (grandchild)	1	1	71
Ignacio Armida Morán (grandchild)	1	1	72
Octaviano Cabrera y Hernández (nephew)	1	1	73
Clara Salas de P. (niece)	2	2	74-75
José Perogordo (nephew)	1	3	76
Faustina Salas C. (niece-religious)	1	1	77
Joaquín Cabrera (nephew)	1	1	78
Carmen Rivero C. (niece)	2	2	79-80
Luis Cabrera y W. (nephew-priest)	1	1	81
Carlota Cabrera y W. (niece-religious)	1	1	82
Ignacio Muriel C. (nephew)	1	1	83
Arturo and Luz Marti (nephew and niece)	1	1	84
Manuela Viadero A. (niece)	1	1	85
María A. y Cartensen (niece)	1	1	86
José Armida y Torres (nephew)	4	8	87-90

The priests who have undertaken the Cause for the Beatification of the Venerable Servant of God in Rome and in Mexico have reviewed this work and believe it will be a favorable means in making Mrs. Armida known in the context of her human and family relationships. Her relatives have also kindly agreed to lend their contribution for the glorification of our Potosinean mystic.

My joy will be complete and my work shall have been rewarded if these letters of my beloved mother are able to put the readers in touch with this transparent and loving soul who brings us into communion with the Lord who filled her soul. May the Lord grant that our lives be filled with His presence.

Dolores Icaza Conrey, R.C.S.C.J.

A MOTHER'S LETTERS

Letters to Her Relatives

To Her Mother Clara Arias y Rivera De Cabrera

Clara Arias y Rivera, a daughter of José Luis Arias and Ignacia Rivera, was born in Santa María del Río, San Luis Potosí, in 1831. On November 23, 1848, she married Octaviano Cabrera y Lacavex, a son of Francisco de Paula Cabrera and María de Jesús Lacavex y Alday, in the parish church (now a cathedral). They had twenty-one children, nine of whom died at birth or very young. The remaining twelve were Manuel, Octaviano, Emilia, José, Luis, Juan, CONCEPCION, Primitivo, Clara, Carlota, Constantino, and Francisco.

In her *Autobiography*, she states:

"My mother was a saint: she was an orphan at two years of age and suffered much; at seventeen she married and we were twelve children, eight boys and four girls; I was number seven, between two boys, Juan and Primitivo, the Jesuit priest.

"My mother instilled in me a love of the Blessed Mother and the Eucharist. She did not let me have friends. She loved me dearly and was sad when I married. Nevertheless, she said my husband was exceptional, that all of them were not like that. She always cried with me in my sorrows and rejoiced in my happiness. She bore many hardships and loved poverty. She had many hidden virtues and unknown martyrdoms. She suffered a stroke and was unconscious for twelve hours. Through our prayers, God permitted her to recover consciousness for the time necessary for her to be able to confess; she had another stroke from which she died. I aided her and put her in her coffin" (loose leaf page 306).

Only one letter of the Venerable Servant of God to her mother is preserved. They both lived in San Luis Potosí until Francisco Armida took his family to Mexico City on the occasion of the Coronation of the Blessed Virgin of Guadalupe on October 12, 1895. Soon afterward, Doña Clara also came to live in the Capital. As the context indicates, this letter is written on the occasion of her mother's short trip to San Luis Potosí. Her mother died in Mexico City on February 20, 1905.

On November 12, 1888, her father, Octaviano Cabrera y Lacavex died in San Luis, and was the first person to be buried in the cemetery "El Saucito" (Willow Tree). Out of humility he asked not to have a tombstone to mark his grave, only a brick with his initials O. de C. which his grandson, Francisco de Paula Cabrera y Dávila changed many years later for a small bronze plaque with the same initials in order to respect the will of his grandfather. Doña Clara also showed a great love for simplicity and poverty even though she had owned seven farms before her marriage: "Labor del Río" (where the bath resort Lourdes is now located), "San José del Jofre," "El Bozo," "Peregrina de Arriba," "Peregrina de Abajo," "La Mesa," and "Jasso."

December 22, 1904

Dearest Mother:

Through Octaviano (1), I learned that you are better and celebrated a simple "posadas" (2) because of being in mourning; you cannot imagine how very simple the posadas here were. I have come down with influenza and only one day did I accompany the feast with music, and once again yesterday. I have not been in bed, and with bronchoquinine and cognac I am getting along.

These days have been really cold and I have taken care of myself. I am all right now, thank God. I am preparing the clothes for the poor child (3), and I appreciate your donation. The Lord will reward you.

This afternoon Clara (4) came and amused me, as always; you know her. With a thousand things to do, the Christmas tree and the gifts for Manuel (5), etc., etc. I am anxious for you to come, you shall see Clarita (6), how cute she is; she already learned the small catechism by heart for her father's saint's day.

Octaviano said you might go to Jesús-María (7), I hope this will not harm you; take good care of yourself, because the winds can be very strong there. I am enthusiastic about going to the Oasis (8) for Midnight Mass. I mean Communion at midnight. I hope there will be no problem going there.

We missed you for the Christmas novena (9); the Nativity set is in the living room with homemade figures; it is really homely, but the children have a good time (10).

Merry Christmas to you, my dear mother; give my regards to Ema and her family, in-laws, nieces and nephews, brothers, etc. and to the "canaries" (11) my remembrance; your daughter embraces you and asks for your blessing.

Concepción

(L.R., Vol. I/2-4)

(1) Octaviano Cabrera y Arias, second son of the marriage of Octaviano Cabrera Lacavex and Clara Arias y Rivera. He was born in San Luis Potosí on February 27, 1851. He married Carmen Hernández y de Ceballos. They had seven children: José Octaviano, Octaviano, Carmen, Mercedes, Joaquín, Luz, and Jesús.

(2) During the Christmas Novena, it is customary to gather in churches and in families to ask for "posada," or lodging, accompanying the Holy Pilgrims, Joseph and Mary; litanies and appropriate songs are sung. Afterwards, piñatas are broken (these are earthen vessels adorned with colored papers and in various shapes, filled with candy and fruit; they are broken with a stick held by a blindfolded person) and other games are played.

(3) The Venerable Servant of God had the custom of sewing clothes to give to poor children at Christmas. By this time she has been a widow for two years and is in a bad economical situation. Her mother, as well as her brother Octaviano, helps her.

(4) Clara Susana Mercedes of the Blessed Trinity Cabrera y Arias, a sister of the Venerable Servant of God, was born in San Luis Potosí on May 24, 1866. She married Doctor Manuel Gallegos. They had only one daughter, Clarita.

(5) Doctor Manuel Gallegos, brother-in-law of Mrs. Armida. He was the family doctor. He celebrated his saint's day on Christmas.

(6) Clara Gallegos Cabrera, born on March 7, 1901, she died on July 6, 1916.

(7) A farm near San Luis Potosí, owned by her brother Octaviano Cabrera Arias. At this site on May 3, 1894, the first Cross of the Apostleship was erected. Mrs. Armida used to go to spend some time there with her children.

(8) The House of the Sisters of the Cross of the Sacred Heart of Jesus, located on 11 Mirto Street, was called "Oasis." Mrs. Armida lived in Number 3 of the same street, right next door to them.

(9) It is a very old, traditional custom to display Nativity sets, artificial reproductions of the Mystery of Bethlehem. The original idea is attributed to Saint Francis of Assisi who is said to have created the first manger scene with living figures in Greccio, in 1223. The first Franciscan missionaries who came to Mexico probably introduced this custom and used it to instruct the natives in the mysteries of Christmas.

(10) Members of the family of Octaviano Cabrera y Arias.

(11) Two old women who had given lessons to the Venerable Servant of God when she was a little girl. They used this nickname for them, because they ate very little, but several times a day.

Her Husband Francisco Armida y García

Her husband, Francisco Armida y García, fourth child of Ildefonso Armida y Verdejo, a Spaniard from Jerez de la Frontera, and Petra García y Delgado, from Cadereyta, Nuevo León. He was born in Monterrey, Nuevo León on March 17, 1858. He met Concepción on December 12, 1875, in San Luis Potosí. For eight years, they maintained a relationship that was pure and inspiring. They were married on November 8, 1884. The marriage was blessed by Canon Luis Arias y Rivera, her mother's brother. They lived in San Luis Potosí until 1895, when they went to reside in Mexico City. He died on September 17, 1901.

No correspondence between them has been preserved, although in Conchita's diary, she records that they wrote to each other during their engagement and she always tried to lead him to God from the very first letter. Once married, they were never separated and so there was no need to write to each other.

The figure of her husband, always a courteous and respectful gentleman, stands out in Concepción's spiritual diary and in her letters to members of her family. It is during the sickness and death of her exemplary and Christian husband and in the faithful remembrance that she maintained of him for years, on anniversaries and memorable dates, that we get a sense of her love for her dear companion.

They had nine children:

FRANCISCO was the first-born and the last one to die. He died on March 3, 1983, which was also the anniversary of his mother's death.

CARLOS was born in San Luis Potosí on March 28, 1887, at 11:45 in the evening in a house on the Plaza de San Juan de Dios. He died on March 10, 1893, at six years of age, at 1 Juárez Street, San Luis Potosí. He is buried in the cemetery of El Saucito.

MANUEL, who was a Jesuit priest, died in Gijón, Spain in 1955.

CONCEPCIÓN, a Sister of the Cross of the Sacred Heart of Jesus, died on December 19, 1925 in Mexico City.

IGNACIO died on June 30, 1979 in Mexico City.

PABLO was born in San Luis Potosí on Saturday, February 9, 1895, at 3:00 in the morning, in Juárez Street, in front of Doña Clara's house (mother of Concepción). He died in Mexico City on June 27, 1913, of typhus and is buried in the Tepeyac cemetery.

SALVADOR died in Mexico City in his home at 8 Ave María Street, on December 2, 1975.

GUADALUPE died on July 18, 1980, also in Mexico City.

PEDRO was born in Mexico City on Monday, February 20, 1899, at 10:00 p.m. in a house on the Paseo de la Reforma. He drowned in the fountain of his house at 7 Alzate Street on April 7, 1903. He was buried in the chapel of the Tepeyac cemetery where they transferred his mortal remains. (1)

(1) The dates appear in her *Autobiography,* loose leaf pages 381-382.

Portrait of Her Husband Francisco
(Taken from her *Autobiography*)
"Thus Was My Husband"

Very good, Christian, gentleman, honest, straightforward, intelligent and with a big heart.

Very sensitive to any misfortune, loving, affectionate with me, an excellent father who had no other amusement than his children: they were his pleasure and he suffered much when they were ill.

He was always very well groomed, refined in his relationships, very generous in his gifts to me; he was a family man, very simple, respectful and refined.

He had a strong and energetic character, that lessened in intensity over time. He had great confidence in me and often talked to me about his business and asked for my opinion although it was not worth much. He was an orderly and methodical man.

From the day following our marriage until he died, he permitted me to receive Holy Communion daily; when we married, I made him promise this. He took care of the children until I came back from church; when he was already very ill, he used to tell me, "Go and receive Communion." As our home was right across the street from the church of the Encarnación, I used to leave just in time for the Consecration and then would rush back quickly to his sickbed.

He never read what I wrote, as he found me sometimes writing my spiritual diary. "Those are spiritual things that I don't understand," he used to tell me.

I had to give in and go with him to the theater and to dances sometimes (more in San Luis). He would never go alone without me.

He proposed to me and told me he loved me on January 16, 1876, and we were married on November 8, 1884. He always treated me with great respect, and in our relationship I tried to make him love the Sacred Heart of Jesus and the Blessed Virgin. On Fridays we never saw each other.

He was very much afraid of death, and when reading to him from [Thomas à] Kempis (*The Imitation of Christ*) the chapter on death often came up and he even believed that I did it on purpose. Two years before his death I did feel he would die soon and I told him so and asked him to do something more for his soul.

The Blessed Virgin took care of me so he would not notice my night penances.

He was a bit jealous.

When I was seriously ill, which did happen several times, he took care of me day and night and would not have anybody watch after me during the night.

He was very vain and when he was dying he asked me to dress him in an old habit of Saint Francis and to give him a second class burial for humility. But there was no old habit, only a new one, and in Tepeyac Cemetery there was only first class interment.

Every Sunday he used to go to the Villa to commend himself to Our Blessed Mother of Guadalupe.

He made a general confession when he was dying and his fear of death was transformed into perfect abandonment to God's will. "I personally believe," he said, "that I am needed now more than ever by my children, but the Lord knows what He is doing, and I want only what He wants."

I helped him at the moment of his death and placed him in the coffin; until he expired, Pancho, Manuel and Concha were at his side. From that moment I consecrated myself to God to be His own forever with my forehead on that of him who had been so good to me (loose leaf pages 379-381).

2

To Her Children Who Were Not in a Religious Order
Francisco, Ignacio, Salvador, and Lupe

June 29, 1928

My dear children, Pancho, Ignacio, Salvador, and Lupe (1):

If I should die, if it pleases the Lord to take me, I ask of you all to continue to live as valiant Christians, full of faith, regardless of what others think, faithfully practicing the teachings of the Church, and being proud to belong to her.

Take care to accomplish the precepts, being generous with Jesus who loves you so, to whom you owe so much and who wishes to save you. I am asking that, by teaching and by example, you pass your faith on to your children at whatever sacrifice in order to give them a Christian education, taking extra care in the formation of their souls, and in their religious instruction.

I cannot insist enough on UNION, UNION, UNION, and on not breaking that union because of temporary upsets or strains that are only human, but using prudence, be of one heart and soul only. I ask you to take care of Salvador (2), his body and his soul. Peace, peace at the price of whatever sacrifice and effort. Be model husbands, and Lupe be a self-sacrificing and saintly wife.

As for the little I own, everything in the business (3) is to be divided equally or, leaving the capital alone, in such a way that at the end of the year the earned interests can be divided in equal parts.

(L.R., Vol. I/6)

(1) In this letter, which is a spiritual testament, Conchita addresses her four children who still lived in Mexico City. Manuel, her son who was a Jesuit, lived in Spain, and the others had already died.

(2) Salvador Armida y Cabrera, who was not yet married.

(3) The business to which Conchita refers is the "Casa Armida," an office supplies business managed by Francisco Armida y Cabrera.

To Her Eldest Son Franciso Armida y Cabrera

Francisco Armida y Cabrera (Pancho) was born in San Luis Potosí in a house on the Plaza de San Juan de Dios. On August 2, 1910, he married Elisa Baz y Duclaud. They had two children: Francisco and María Cecilia. Francisco had four children, and María Cecilia, already deceased, a daughter and two grandchildren.

Pancho died on March 3, 1983.

Mrs. Armida writes about him in her *Autobiography*:

"The Birth of Pancho, my first child.

"On Monday, September 28, 1885, my first child was born at nine in the evening. I offered him up to the Lord with all my heart, before and after I held him in my arms. The Lord granted that I could feed him for eight months and then had to wean him out of necessity. Afterwards I experienced many difficulties: he did not accept a wet nurse and with donkey's milk (the most like my own) he got through his preweaning period.

"I suffered a lot during the birth and breast-feeding of this child.

"A silly thing: I wanted at all costs for him to say 'mamá' (mom) but much to my regret his first word was 'gato' (cat).

"This boy never did anything that merited a scolding: a very good student, intelligent, straightforward, honorable and dependable, responsible. He had a strong character but also a good heart. It seems the Lord calls him to married life" (pp. 114-115).

Conchita had a very close relationship with this son, for whom she had a special fondness.

He was only sixteen when his father died, and he became head of the family. He set to work with great success. With his cousins of the Muriel family, he founded a business for the sale of typewriters and other office supplies, "Casa Armida," which is still in business. He acted as an agent for foreign manufacturers, often traveling to foreign countries because of his business. He provided employment for his brothers and brother-in-law, Carlos Lafarga.

He managed to pull through the economic crisis of the years 1930-1933. An honest and upright man, he was generous with the poor. Every year he donated special gifts to his employees at Christmas.

He was the last survivor and died on the same date as his mother, March 3. During his last years he gave more time to prayer and received Holy Communion daily. He went to the parish church in Coyoacán barefoot early in the morning to attend Mass. He lived in the Plaza de Santa Catarina in a beautiful colonial house.

3

August 2, 1910

To my son

Pancho, my beloved son:

Not only one but a thousand blessings would I tenderly send your way today, enveloping you in them and in all of the blessings of heaven.

Through God's favor I have a grace which few mothers can recount: that of taking you to the altar and presenting you to the saintly wife the Blessed Mother has chosen for you, as unblemished as I received you myself. What a fortune to arrive as a lily, as an angel, to receive the grace of matrimony: This above all will make your father smile in heaven, as he wishes you a chaste marriage, which he too, will bless with affection. You enter a new state of life, son of my soul; you can also be chaste in it, sacrificing yourself and forging souls, if the Lord provides you with children, for His Glory. Let us bless God for His countless gifts.

You have been a model son and I hope you will also be a husband as Christian, as honorable, as loving and noble as your father was: in that way you will make Elisa truly happy, as she, with great devotion and first love is going to unite her life to your own.

I had always prayed that the Lord would give you a wife who would understand you, who, with her virtues, would sweeten your character, who would cultivate your religious feelings, who could be your companion in this exile, who would wipe away your tears, who would help you endure life's sorrows and appease your grief and help you to remove the thorns in your path.

God has listened to my humble prayers for He never fails to

hear a mother's plea, and so you have found this ideal upon earth.

You are going to receive her today from the hands of the Holy Church, she is a sacred gift: she is going to be the mother of your children. Respect her, love her and appreciate her, and then she will be whatever you wish her to be.

Avoid the least quarrel and do not stop at any sacrifice to have peace in your home and with her family. It is better to bend than to break; with prudence, education and certain common sense, many troubles can be avoided. Oh, my son! Never forget that everything you are, all that you have and the happiness you now enjoy, you owe to the good Jesus Who has loved you with such tenderness! From how many dangers He has delivered you! How He has cared for you since you became an orphan! Truly Divine Providence has taken care of you, has covered you with its shadow and led you gently, opening new horizons for your future. Be grateful, my son: recognize with gratitude the fatherly tenderness of God over you and demonstrate your gratitude by your actions, and never be ashamed of being a good Christian.

You have been the favored child of Mary: never cease to call upon her; never forget to pray your rosary, and in your joys and in your sorrows, let her always be your Mother and the Mother of your children. Depend on her love to make your home a heavenly one. Before putting an end to this letter, I am going to give you a little advice poured forth from the heart that most loves you on earth.

Keep your faith even in the great burdens of your life: the religion you profess, the only true one, must be your shield and your pride, and instruct in it the children God wills to give you, teaching them to love it and respect it as the greatest thing upon earth.

Direct Elisa with sweetness, preferring persuasion and good reason to force and authority, which cause coolness. Remember that in married life, it is very dangerous to extinguish the flame of love, respect, and esteem.

Do not invite friends to your home frequently, but do not be a jealous husband; mistrustful husbands do not honor their own dignity.

Do not be too familiar with your wife's relatives: a sincere respect, dignified and constant, will keep you from arguments, even though you might have to give in.

Never use harsh words with Elisa, much less offensive ones; keep silent during the first impulses and you will never repent for having done so. Be dignified with everyone but never haughty. Keep on being honest under every circumstance. Do not soil your soul with business deals that extort your fellowmen. You understand me. May your soul be always clean — poverty does not soil or shame one — and you will be happy.

Participate in honest recreations and always accompanied by your wife: if she is ill, do not abandon her for your friends; these engagements would make her suffer, even though she would have the prudence of not letting you know.

I tell you that, in marriage, although it is necessary to have social relationships, it is more important to love your own home and to render it hospitable, embellishing it with flowers, controlling your own inclinations and dedicating yourself to your children through self-denial.

May your home, dear Pancho, be a model of Christian homes where the Lord reigns and a worldly atmosphere does not enter; where the peace and happiness that are born from the accomplishment of one's duty, be settled there.

Take care to receive the Sacraments frequently and never abandon them under any circumstance in your life. Elisa is a good Christian and will tend to those practices of piety which, even seemingly small, are important in the formation of the family.

Never spend more than you have, not even all that you earn: thrift helps marriages avoid a lot of trouble. But do not be avaricious; aim for a happy medium, maintaining a decent and fitting social standing, not living in luxury, even if you become rich. Let the poor be considered one of your ordinary expenses, and God will not fail you.

Don't limit your piety to exterior observances but rather practice the virtues, being patient in adversity, resigned to the adverse events of life "because if we receive from the Lord so many goods, why should we not also receive the sufferings He desires to send us?"

Never leave your brothers if I should no longer be here; look after them as your father would; you represent him before them: help them in the future, above all their souls, and the Lord will bless you.

I hope the Lord will still leave me upon earth to enjoy your happiness, but as you are going away and I am so often ill, I thought about writing this advice for the future; if you follow it you shall be very joyful.

Forgive me, my son, for all the bad example I might have given you, and do not follow it.

I bless you again with all my soul in my name and in the name of your father. I would also be so pleased if on this happy day in which God is going to bless your union by means of a saintly Bishop, who loves you so (1), you would wear this watch your father wore until the last day of his life: accept it as a gift of great value for the memories it holds.

So then be joyful in your marriage and you surely will be so as long as you accomplish God's will and keep it in the center of your heart.

Your humble mother who blesses you.

Concepción
(L.R., Vol. I/12-19)

---

(1) Ramón Ibarra y González, Archbishop of Puebla. Father Primitivo Cabrera Arias, S.J., celebrated the Holy Mass.

To Her Daughter-in-Law Elisa Baz y Duclaud
Wife of Her Son Francisco

This is the only letter to her daughter-in-law, Elisa Baz Duclaud, that has been preserved, a fact that is easily explained as both of them lived in Mexico City.

Elisa was born on October 29, 1886. She married Mrs. Armida's eldest son on August 2, 1910. They had, as we have already said, two children.

Francisco Armida Baz was born on April 15, 1917. On April 14, 1945, he married Beda Muñoz Castillo. They had four children, María Concepción, Beda, Francisco Manuel, and Alejandro José.

María Cecilia was born also in Mexico City on March 6, 1921. On March 1, 1945, she married Leendert van Rhijn, a Dutchman, born on August 13, 1905. They had an only daughter, Patricia Guadalupe, born on August 12, 1949. On March 1, 1968, Patricia Guadalupe married Antonio Castellanos. They are parents of two children, Federico and Elisa, born respectively on September 2, 1968, and on February 23, 1972.

Doña Elisa seemed to have been somewhat attracted to social life. The Venerable Servant of God tried to draw her daughter-in-law toward a life of a greater piety. In the last years of her life, she did give more attention to religion. She wrote some devout poetry.

This letter discretely reflects the values Mrs. Armida actually lived in her own home: her desire to please her husband and to make her home agreeable to him, her attention to those details that could make her husband and children happy, her yearning to elevate their aspirations and hopes to supreme values, especially eternal ones.

3a

August 12, 1911

Elisa, my beloved daughter:

Because of the great affection that I have for you, I am going to take the liberty of giving you some advice. I do not want to hurt your feelings, and consider that I am speaking secretly and only to your heart.

You possess many virtues and qualities with which the Lord has endowed you, and it is your obligation to exploit and enhance them for your own good and for that of those who surround you. You must be a saint in your home. Pancho is a very worthy man and will never be satisfied with a wife who does not possess solid virtues.

[…] You need to be always occupied doing some handwork; this is very much appreciated in a woman, very proper for a married woman and very much to Pancho's liking. Never get up in the morning after Pancho does, but join him for breakfast. Never seat your lady friends between Pancho and yourself. Always arrive home before Pancho does. Before eating, go and see if everything is set in the kitchen and in the dining room. Pray the rosary with the servants.

Dedicate yourself totally to pleasing and complimenting Pancho in every way you possibly can. Be very frugal and orderly in your expenditures.

Receive Holy Communion every day, this I urge you with all my heart: in this practice you will find strength, virtues and everything you need in order to be a model Christian woman and wife. Talk to Pancho about substantial and serious things. He does not like vain and trivial subjects.

Set your heart above worldly things — fashions and clothes,

etc. — and if the Lord gives you children, educate them not to follow the common ways of the world, but to save their souls from vanity, inspiring in them from their youth elevated thoughts, upright and divine viewpoints, delivering them from the world and all evil.

My Licha: Pancho is a real treasure. Keep him within the reliquary of his home and make it pleasant through your virtues, tenderness, prudence, and order.

I ask you to do all you can for my poor sons. All you do for them I will not forget in heaven, where I will be waiting for you.

Your humble mother,

Concepción
(L.R., Vol. I/88-90)

To Her Son, the Jesuit Priest,
Manuel Armida y Cabrera

Manuel Armida y Cabrera, her third son, was born on Rosario Street in San Luis Potosí, on Monday, October 28, 1889, when the Angelus bells were ringing (*Autobiography*, loose leaf page 381).

"At that hour José Camacho, a priest, died; and as soon as I learned this, I offered my little boy to the Lord to take his place before the altar. I really gave him with all my heart. After this baby was born, I remained very ill, still I was able to feed him until he walked. Manuel always had a happy character, docile and humble, and since he was a very small child he had a very strong attraction to virtue, to things belonging to the Church. Enlightened, he had a special detachment from the world and its vanities, superior to his age. He entered the Society of Jesus in 1906 at the age of seventeen (*Autobiography* I, p. 44).

"I remember he must have been about seven years old when one day, at dinner time, as all the children were around him, their father told them to hurry and grow up soon so that they could help him with the household expenses, and Manuel quickly answered: 'I will help you, yes, but in the spiritual part, in what touches the soul, because I was not born to earn money which is vanity and dust.' Pancho and I looked at each other and were surprised at that response.

"He had a period of terrible scruples: he was always very pious and, with disregard for people's opinion, very naive and simple. He was the most loving of all my children, maybe even exaggeratedly so. The Lord called him. He heard my prayers and his; and from the time he began to talk, we asked for the great grace of a religious vocation. At his First Communion and on the great feasts of the Church, he renewed this petition with fervor: and the Lord heard him, I say, taking him to the Society of Jesus on November 12, 1906, where he took his vows on December 8, 1908 at nineteen years and eleven months of age" (*Autobiography* I, pp. 136-138).

He was sent by his Superiors to Spain and offered the sacrifice of not returning to his native land. During her trip to the Holy Land and Rome in 1913, they saw each other in Loyola. He died in Gijón, Spain, at the Academy of Mary Immaculate in 1955.

There are 58 letters of the Venerable Servant of God to her son Manuel, a Jesuit priest, of which we have selected 21. They are among the most affectionate letters in all her correspondence. The two were very close because they shared a similar religious sensitivity and love for Jesus. In these letters she talks about everything: news, sorrows, joys, her concern for his brothers; news about the political, religious, social, and economic situation back home; she also talks about the works of the Cross which were so close to her heart; gives him some spiritual advice along with home remedies for certain illnesses. Her great maternal tenderness as well as her prudence in consoling and encouraging her religious and priestly son, so inclined to scruples and discouragement, are clearly revealed in these letters.

Manuel's heroism in asking to be sent to Spain and remaining there, far from his mother, brothers and his country, has provided us with this rich correspondence between them.

May 26, 1906

My dear son Manuel:

I am so anxious to see you very early tomorrow (1) to give you many gifts. I am sending you a rich egg cake so you may have an early supper.

You must have begun the novena to the Holy Spirit. Pray it fervently so that I can trust that God will open a way for you, you shall see. I wish this even more than you do, but faith with good deeds will not leave us disappointed.

I am very happy with your behavior, and we shall talk tomorrow.

In the meantime your mother gives you her blessing.

Concepción
(L.R., Vol. I/100)

(1) It seems that Manuel had been making a closed spiritual retreat to discern his vocation. On the closing day, it was a custom to celebrate with those who had made the spiritual exercises.

5

November 27, 1906

My dear son Manuel:

I have just received your letter which I was anxiously expecting and I prayed the Te Deum with all my heart upon receiving it.

Blessed be God that He has given you light and with it has let you know His will. That is the only thing I desire: His holy will to be accomplished and for you to accomplish it in every detail. If you do so as you say, you will be happy in this life and in the next one.

So I unite myself to your happiness with all my heart and I send you my blessing which, although not worth much, is nevertheless a blessing from a mother and it will draw the blessings from heaven upon you.

I have fervently asked the Blessed Virgin that you may be a perfect novice and a saintly religious. From now on think only about God and of how you may sacrifice yourself for Him.

You will let me know what I must send you in the way of clothing, expenses, etc.

Until the 20th, unless the Lord desires otherwise, we shall be in Mixcoac (24 Campana Street), although it would be good and more profitable for your soul, I believe, if you write as little as possible.

Pray for me, I do need it, and for your brothers who send their love to you and unite themselves to your happiness (1).

Your mother who blesses you in the name of the Father and of the Son and of the Holy Spirit.

Concepción
(L.R., Vol. I/106)

(1) It seems that Manuel has decided upon his vocation. His mother asks what he needs for his entry into the Society of Jesus.

On November 12, Volume 24, page 200, she writes in her *Spiritual Diary*: "Anniversary of the death of my father (Octaviano Cabrera Lacavex). Manuel left for the Novitiate of the Society of Jesus, 'El Llano,' to make the spiritual exercises and to decide his vocation, either for the Society, for the Cross, or for the world."

These were very painful days for her because of the natural maternal grief due to the separation from her son, and for spiritual reasons: she had prayed and hoped and dreamed that he would form part of the future Congregation of the Religious of the Cross which would afterward take the name of Missionaries of the Holy Spirit, through the suggestion of His Holiness Saint Pius X.

6

December 9, 1906

O Crux spes unica!

My dear son Manuel:

I read with the interest you might suppose, the account in your long letter (1) about your decision regarding your holy vocation: I have blessed the Lord a thousand times because He deigned to open a path for you and filled your soul with peace.

Afterward I received your other letters, along with the watch, etc., asking for your certificate of baptism and confirmation which I am sending to you today; and later your other letter including the express ticket.

I do see the Lord's grace operating in your heart and I do not know how to thank Him for His blessings. How can we respond to such goodness? Give yourself with all your soul to the Lord, without looking back and reclaiming yourself: forget creatures and above all forget yourself: empty yourself of everything that is not God or that does not conduct you to Him, and live in obedience, humility, and self-denial. Die to yourself so that Jesus alone lives and reigns in your soul. I cannot imagine a religious who is not saintly and one must not give things to God only halfway: life is so short when one wants to sacrifice it for Him out of love, so be generous with Him.

It will happen, and perhaps soon, that temptations and struggles may come to upset you, but stand firmly and always love the Cross in whatever manner it comes up to you, because it is always kind to the heart that sees the sacred will of God wrapped in its seeming ruggedness.

Clearly my mother's heart has suffered, but I am happy in being able to offer the Lord the sacrifice which is in favor of your soul, a thousand times more precious to me than your body. Yes, pray always, pray for me since you are more or less not mindless of all my toils, obligations, and needs.

I have communicated your decision to the whole family and they will pray for you. Your brothers will write to you soon. I will do so only in case of necessity to answer when you are allowed to write to me.

Do not remember me except before the Tabernacle, that is, in your prayers. I have made the Lord a complete gift of Manuel, and therefore your love, your thoughts and everything you are, belongs only to Him. I have also placed you under Mary's veil; you have already been there since you were a child; she is your Mother, love her without limit, like Saint Stanislaus (2).

So keep your feet on earth but raise your soul, your life and your whole heart up to heaven.

I am sending you a cape if they let you use it, for I believe that the coat you took along with you will not be useful now. I am also sending three shirts, three undershirts, three underwear, six pairs of socks, and six handkerchiefs.

Primitivo (3) told me to send a half dozen of each item. This good brother left on Monday for the Tarahumara. I am envious of him! Pray that he may save many souls.

Your humble mother who blesses you.

Concepción
(L.R., Vol. I/101-105)

(1) In her *Spiritual Diary* on November 27, 1906 (24/227), the Venerable Servant of God says: "Manuel, my son, writes me that he has been admitted to the Society of Jesus and that he is going to begin his novitiate, that he prays the Te Deum, and that he is HAPPY. I offered this letter to Jesus trembling, I read it kneeling, and a stab went through my heart. In the middle of tears that unwillingly flowed from my eyes, I prayed the Te

Deum, I THANKED the Lord, first, for the great favor He bestowed on my son and after, because He so humbled me" (She had wanted him to become part of the Congregation of the Missionaries of the Holy Spirit). On December 1, 1906 (24/254): "Jesus, Jesus, my Jesus, I renounce this so loved child giving him up to you in the SOCIETY FOREVER! My love makes this donation today, humbly asking you to accept it with benevolence. Amen."

In her *Spiritual Diary* (30/179) on July 10, 1908, she records: "I received a card from Manuel's Master of Novices and then another one from Fr. Ipiña, in which both of them told me that on the 14th, my son Manuel would arrive here and would only stay for a day; and that he would continue his trip to Veracruz, where he would embark for Spain on the 16th. He will continue his Novitiate in Loyola and take his vows. Will he ever come back...?" "July 14: Manuel arrived and my motherly heart beat expecting him.... I was anxious to embrace him, feel his heart near to mine that has so suffered for him. Finally I saw him.... he stayed only one hour in the 'Oasis' with Concha. I cannot describe my feelings on seeing them together.... I in the middle of my two religious for Jesus."

On January 23, 1914 (*Spiritual Diary* 38/594) she has the pleasure of seeing him in Irún, and to accompany him to Loyola and on to San Sebastián. On January 30: "We talked, laughed, cried praising the Lord. Manuel very learned and spiritual. We recalled his childhood, his vocation, etc." And on the 31st: "Poor Manuel, he has enjoyed everything so much!"

At last on June 12, 1920, Manuel writes to her communicating his decision to stay in Spain and never return to Mexico. She copies the letter of her son into her *Spiritual Diary* (43/81). Her answer to his letter is the one we publish.

She confesses: "Yes, this letter brought tears to my heart, but with God's help, I accepted and offered up the sacrifice, offering not to see him upon earth, even if I could go to Spain. I renounced the joy of hearing his Mass when he is ordained, of hearing him when he preaches, of him giving me Holy Communion, of going to him for Confession, and of him helping me at the moment of my death, perhaps, by giving me the last absolution." This is the dream of every mother of a priest. Both of them were making a great sacrifice. She encourages him in this generous dedication to his ministry. "May the Lord accept my poor and imperfect sacrifice that makes my soul bleed. I am not worthy of such a son. I answered thus."

(2) St. Stanislaus Kostka was born in Poland on October 28, 1550. In 1567 he went to Rome to enter the Novitiate of the Society of Jesus. In 1568 he became ill and died on the Feast of the Assumption of the Blessed Virgin as a fervent novice devout to Mary and the Most Blessed Eucharist.

(3) Her brother, Father Primitivo Cabrera y Arias, S.J., priest and missionary in Tarahumara and in Los Mixes, Oaxaca, Mexico.

7

Answer to Manuel's letter, June 12, 1920
(*Spiritual Diary* 43/81-84)

My dear son Manuel:

What can I say after receiving your letter with the news that I was waiting for, knowing you as I know you? Just that I gave infinite thanks to God (even though drenched in tears) for having inspired and having given you the strength to make this great sacrifice. I immediately went behind the Tabernacle and I put your letter there, right next to it, and I told the Lord that, with all my heart, I accepted this sacrifice that so profoundly touched me.

On the next day I carried your letter over my heart when I went to receive Holy Communion, so as to confirm my complete acceptance.

Happy are you, my son, because you placed Jesus above flesh and blood and by an act of faith lifted yourself far above the earth.

The little good you received from me during your formation was not mine, but God's, who chose you for Himself from your earliest years with an infinite predilection, giving you a religious vocation.

I do not know whether you received a letter from me in which, foreseeing your sacrifice, I told you that Mexico was in great need of workers; that there are many regions with Indians who are still pagans where the Kingdom of Christ could be extended through great sacrifice and denial. For instance, in the Tarahumara (1) and now near Múzquiz (2), where your uncle Primitivo is seeing about establishing a new Jesuit residence there.

The new Father Provincial Crevelli is very much interested in seeing to the evangelization of these areas. I told you that, should you come, if you so desired I would not come to see you, if you would only tell me so.

Now obedience has sanctioned your desire and this is undoubtedly God's will, which, with all my heart, I accept, venerate and LOVE.

Love achieves all things! Love is giving. When this donation is not yet perfect it is desire; when it is accomplished, love is peace; when it is eternal it is bliss. To give is love's essential function and whoever loves does not look upon himself and does not pamper himself! For a soul that really loves the Lord, of what importance are honors, wealth, social position, the future, suffering, and even death itself? The important thing is that Jesus is pleased, even though the soul suffers; that He rejoices, even though the soul grieves; that He smiles even though the soul weeps. When a person truly loves, the "ego" disappears and dies so that Jesus alone may live within the heart.

"Truly," a soul used to say, "Love is a death and a life; the most complete death, and the happiest life." O, Manuel, son of my heart! The greatest thing that exists after God, the only divine task that a creature may accomplish, is to love Him and give Him glory, offering himself up to the Lord.

Saint Ignatius' motto A.M.D.G. (3) is the supreme formula of love. How unknown is this love upon earth, but happy are those who have received that enlightenment of the Cross.

For the world to love is to enjoy yourself; it thinks in its selfishness that love consists above all in receiving consolation, satisfaction, etc. It is exactly the contrary: love is nourished by GIVING, by self-sacrifice, with the holy fuel of suffering.

Enough sermonizing, let me just conclude by saying I congratulate you again a thousand times because you have found the true way to heaven. Be always generous with the Lord out of pure love and you shall always be happy on earth and in our true Home! Your brothers are very sad, and say they will go to see you; ask the Lord that you may find me in heaven, although I am very far from being worthy of it.

I end with regards from your brothers and my approval and my blessing.

Your mother, happy in the midst of her sorrow, hugs you.

Concepción
(L.R., Vol. I/108-113)

(1) The region of the Tarahumara is a mission land, located in the Sierra Madre Occidental. It includes part of the States of Sonora, Chihuahua and Sinaloa. The natives are from the Nahua race, related to the Pima. They were evangelized but went back to paganism and witchery. They use inebriating herbs and drinks.

(2) Perhaps a part of Coahuila that took its name from Melchor Múzquiz (1790-1844), who was originally from Santa Rosa, Coahuila.

(3) A.M.D.G. is the motto of the Society of Jesus, "Ad Maiorem Dei Gloriam" — For the greater glory of God — from St. Ignatius of Loyola, their founder.

8

August 15, 1931

Veni Sancte!

My dear Manuel:

I have not written to you because I have had some trouble with the glands in my throat and with my kidneys, but I am better, thanks be to God.

I have been thinking about you and poor Spain; Soviet influence. What a pity! I am anxious to know where all of this is going to end; Primitivo told me today that Father General was asking the Jesuits not to leave Spain.

Over here, too, the religious question is becoming worse; the devil does not want celebrations for the Fourth Centenary of the apparition of Our Lady of Guadalupe. The Masons are furious because of the thousands and thousands of pilgrims who are coming from all over the Republic. We have reason to think we are going back again to something like the age of the catacombs. In Veracruz, there was a shooting in a Church filled with four hundred children taking catechism lessons: a priest died (1) and two more were injured including a young lady; a little boy also died. They are pursuing Bishop Guízar (2) to kill him.

They say Calles (3) will come in again as President and we fear a revolution. Three problems: revolution, the religious question, and the financial issue. The decrees Calles has issued are terrible: The prohibition of the circulation of gold; the fall of silver, etc. Countless businesses will go broke. Your brothers lost 200,000 pesos because they sold in gold and they are being paid in silver. They buy in dollars that have gone up four and a half times and this is also a great loss.

Pancho (4) went to New York to ask the factories for a moratorium. It was given to him but when he got back, he found this disaster which was the last straw and he is at the point of bankruptcy.

This month he will have worked thirty years to end up in this very distressing situation.

Bankruptcy is a civil death; for eight years he would not be able to own anything; it is very hard for him with his creditors because with this general depression they cannot sell anything yet the expenses continue.

He has kidney and liver trouble and great mental exhaustion. I am very worried about his condition. He goes to Communion daily and prays and begs and abandons himself to God's will, all the while bleeding. With this depression, Ignacio (5), Salvador (6), and Carlos (7), could be on the street and there is no employment: Sommer (8) has dismissed many employees; in one day they terminated eighteen. There is no way to start something new. So each one of my sons is a worry for me. Lupe's (9) health is precarious. Octaviano (10) has lost 400,000 pesos and the brewery (11) is on the point of collapsing. In the end, the situation does not threaten me personally: it worries me because of your brothers and their families, but I pray God's will may be accomplished in everything. Undoubtedly it must be the best for us, as everything that happens occurs through God's love.

Pray for all of them and ask God to open new ways, and that they do not lose their faith; their souls are the most important thing.

And now I have spoken to you of nothing but business, another time I will speak of spiritual matters.

Work on your sanctification, do not be pessimistic: love and sacrifice, abandoned to God's will.

Everyone sends you their love and asks you to pray for them. Receive my blessing sending me yours.

(L.R., Vol. I/128-130)

(1) Father Darío Acosta, newly ordained priest. He was beatified in Rome by Pope John Paul II on November 25, 1992 in a group of twenty-five Mexican martyrs.

(2) Rafael Guízar Valencia, Bishop of Veracruz, who heroically was able to keep his Seminary open during the religious persecution. The Cause of his Canonization has been promoted in Rome. He has already been named Blessed on January 29, 1995, by His Holiness John Paul II.

(3) Plutarco Elías Calles. President of the Mexican Republic from 1924 to 1928, who continued even afterwards to have an influence on politics. He was born in Guaymas, Sonora, in 1877 and died in Mexico City in 1945.

(4) Her son, Francisco Armida Cabrera.

(5) Her son, Ignacio Armida Cabrera.

(6) Her son, Salvador Armida Cabrera.

(7) Her son-in-law, Carlos Lafarga Aragón, husband of her daughter Guadalupe.

(8) The commercial firm Sommer Herrmann, a large hardware store in Mexico City.

(9) Guadalupe Armida Cabrera, Concepción's daughter.

10) Octaviano Cabrera Arias, Concepción's brother.

11) The Brewery was called "El Monopolio," in San Luis Potosí.

9

March 9, 1932

Veni Sancte!

My dear son Manuel:

You may realize the great sorrow I have felt upon receiving your letter with the latest news (1). I was deeply touched, but at the same time I congratulate you because Our Lord has considered you worthy of suffering for His cause. Happy are you my child for receiving such a great gift! Give thanks to the Lord with all your heart and be happy in your present situation (sent by a loving Father) be it what it may.

I hope you received a bill of exchange for 500 pesetas, and I will soon send you another one for your necessary expenses. I wish the circumstances were different so I could send you more. The Lord will help me, while your situation improves.

We are also suffering here. They have left only twenty-five priests (there used to be three hundred) in all of Mexico City and just think about the troubles they have to endure. Communism is more threatening than the Government, and only God can save us.

The chaos is worldwide and is a chastisement from the Lord; far from becoming any better, public morality keeps getting worse, immodesty reigns along with so many crimes, all sorts of fearful and dreadful crimes.

The Pope (2) told the Bishop Delegate (3) to accept the twenty-five priests fearing something worse; but he made it clear that he acquiesced only on account of the tyranny. Some persons did not like this, but obedience comes before all else.

Your brothers will keep on struggling so as not to close the business for just one more month, but nobody is buying or paying for anything, and this is a disaster; the most probable thing to happen is a liquidation sale. Poor boys! But God shall help them since we have placed all our trust in Him.

I will write to you soon; for the present I will just send you these lines. Ignacio has a bad case of the flu, we have all come down with it; there is an epidemic here in Mexico City and in the States.

Take good care of yourself; do not worry; abandon yourself completely into God's hands and embrace your precious cross as "the Cross carries those who carry it with love."

Your brothers are worried about you and ask me to tell you so; they send their regards until they themselves are able to write.

You mother, who loves you so, blesses you and envies you.

Concepción
(L.R., Vol. I/131-132)

(1) Manuel, in Spain, is suffering on account of the civil war and religious persecution.
(2) Pope Pius XI.
(3) Archbishop and Apostolic Delegate Leopoldo Ruíz y Flores.

10

March 23, 1932

Veni Sancte!

My dear son Manuel:

I am very worried because I have had no news from you. I sent you a bill of exchange for 500 pesetas to the Bank of Bilbao and I do not know whether you received it or not; the letter was sent to Mrs. Rubiera. Maybe you are no longer in Oviedo. Let me know how you are, at least through a post card.

I have seen in the *Hormiga de Oro* some buildings that the [Spanish] government expropriated from the Society of Jesus at Loyola, which made me especially sad. What a pity!

The Sisters from the Society of Saint Thérèse told me that in Oviedo, the Sister Superior of the "Besada Saint Thérèse School" is Guadalupe Mora, a niece of the deceased Bishop of Mexico (1). Go and pay her a visit for me. From Barcelona Mother Superior General and Mother Saturnina (2) are going to recommend you to her, that they might take care of you and give you whatever you need. Please go, as I promised them you would; do it for my peace of mind.

Here the situation is calmer. The French colony has had its church returned, and they continue to ask for more.

When Mass is said, people flow out onto the street and traffic is stopped. There have been spiritual retreats generally in homes and in churches; they call them "conferences." God helps His own and does not let them down.

As for you, how are you? Very brave, very confident, very generous and at peace? I expect this of you and pray the Lord that you profit by these crosses for your soul's sake: why not, if Jesus loves you so that He wishes to give you a drop from His chalice, a thorn from His crown? Courage! The Cross carries him who carries it with love. Who would fear anything at Jesus' side and in His Company? LOVE HIM A GREAT DEAL, LET HIM LOVE YOU, BOLDLY ASK HIM TO LOVE YOU, CARE FOR YOU, EMBRACE YOU, HUG YOU TO HIS LOVING HEART, BECAUSE HIS DELIGHT IS BEING WITH THE SONS OF MEN. Become a little child, throw yourself into His arms! It pleases Him that we need Him, that we request, that we confide in His tenderness and in His love! The poorer we are, the more we have a right to His caresses and His graces! Blessed persecution that opens for you a great horizon to suffer more, to confide more, to love Jesus without measure, because of the fondness of His love! Oh how good Jesus is! In His arms what can you fear? Inside His Heart, what can you lack? Oh, how good Jesus is: He looks for pretexts to pour out His favors upon us! Who can ever outdo His thoughtfulness and His incomparable sweetness? Can one find a more refined sensitivity than that suffered by a loving heart, a priestly soul? Does love ask for a rest, or suffering a pause, since its joy is to suffer for the loved one? Do not measure the height of your Calvaries, nor the weight or the dimension of your Cross: forget yourself, your true sorrow being solely that of seeing Jesus offended, insulted and persecuted. All our martyrdoms are like shooting stars before the Cross of Jesus.

Be a victim for the guilty; forgive and forget; complete Jesus' passion in your own heart. I envy you, because persecution is a sign of those who are chosen; no wonder Saint Ignatius requested it for his sons.

Write to me, even if it's only a postcard, so I can hear from you. I want to send you another 500 pesetas, but I do not know where to send them, since you have not let me know whether you received the others.

Keep on praying for your brothers: the time has come for all of us to be put to the test. Blessed be God!

Pray for Lupe (3); she is expecting a little angel in June, and she always has trouble; and Chabela (4) in April. Where am I to send you the journal *La Cruz*? (5) Be very holy, son of mine; profit from your daily sufferings since these pass away, but the CONSOLATION OF CONSOLING JESUS IS ETERNAL.

Your poor mother embraces you, blesses you with all her soul and wishes you a very holy Christmas.

Concepción
(L.R., Vol. I/133-135)

(1) José Mora y del Río, Archbishop of Mexico.

(2) Mother Saturnina Jassá y Fontcuberta, Theresian religious, whose Cause of Beatification is in Rome. Ramón Ibarra y González, Archbishop of Puebla, asked her to live for a time with the Sisters of the Cross of the Sacred Heart of Jesus to teach them about religious life.

(3) Guadalupe Armida Cabrera de Lafarga.

(4) Isabel Morán Bolaños Cacho, wife of her son Ignacio.

(5) The journal of spirituality, *La Cruz*, was founded by Father Félix de Jesús Rougier, M.Sp.S. in 1921 and faithfully kept in print by Father José Guadalupe Treviño, M.Sp.S. The Missionaries of the Holy Spirit continue to publish it to this very day.

11

May 17, 1932

Veni Sancte!

My dear son Manuel:

Before I forget — as I always do — I received the pictures, the money you sent back to me on time; I was hurt that you would not accept such a small amount. The spiritual reasons you give soothe me and I am delighted to see in you a great desire to resemble Jesus. Transform yourself in Him, my son; everything else is straw, details. I cannot imagine a priest who is not another Jesus, and even less in the Society of Jesus; this is what I pray for you, that your transformation in Him at the moment of the Mass is perpetuated and that day and night you are truly Jesus.

Father Félix (1) thanks you for your congratulations on the Decretum Laudis and the Constitutions (2). On Pentecost, that is, the day before yesterday, the first General Chapter took place. The Pope (3) sent a wire wishing them the best and offering his prayers for the Chapter. Father Félix was elected and, as Father Vicar, Edmundo Iturbide (4), grandson or great grandson of the Emperor Iturbide (5); he is a very saintly man and has been in Rome for a number of years. There are already almost fifty priests here, and I have been told that those coming from Rome are Doctors of Theology and Canon Law.

I am awfully sorry that this letter will not arrive on time for your saint's day, but you must be sure you will be in my heart and in my humble prayers. Nine days, all for you. Your brothers are going to write to you.

Mother Saturnina tells me that they have asked Mother Mora

(6) to help you all she can. They are so good! Thank you for the interesting newspapers you sent to me. May the Lord reward you! How very beautiful and great the Society of Jesus is! Be worthy of such a Mother! Let's hope, God willing, that the dark clouds will soon pass and everything will return to normal. Here we are struggling, but we keep going ahead anyway.

Nacho and Chabela (7) are going to send you some pictures and baptismal cards of Jacobito (8). Ask the Lord that Lupe (9) will be all right at the end of June: it is a worry for me.

Your brothers have been ruined by the rising price of the dollar. Be it as the Lord wills!

Give me your blessing and receive my best benediction that I send to you with all my heart and soul.

When I was in San Luis, they forced me to have my picture taken; I had not been in one since that group photo we took with you! It is very seldom that all four brothers are able to get together; the only ones left of the twelve! (10) I am sending the picture to you.

Concepción
(L.R., Vol. I/138-139)

(1) Father Félix Rougier y Olanier, a French priest, initially a member of the Society of Mary, and a missionary in Colombia. When he learned about the Works of the Cross through Concepción Cabrera de Armida, their inspiration, he founded, after ten years of heroic obedience to his Marist superiors, the Congregation of the Missionaries of the Holy Spirit, the fifth of the Works of the Cross. He was born in Meilhaud, Auvergne, France, on December 17, 1859 and was baptized on the following day. He died in Mexico City on January 10, 1938. His Cause for Beatification has been introduced in Rome. On July 1, 2000, he was declared Venerable by His Holiness Pope John Paul II.

(2) The Missionaries of the Holy Spirit were founded in Mexico City on December 25, 1914, behind the locked doors of the small Chapel of the Roses in the Villa de Guadalupe because of the revolution and religious persecution. On June 10, 1931, Rome granted them the Decretum Laudis and the Approval of their Constitutions "ad experimentum" for seven years. They now have all of the necessary approvals for their Institute.

(3) His Holiness Pope Pius XI (Achille Ratti).

(4) Father Edmundo Iturbide Reygondaud. One of the first members of the new Congregation of the Missionaries of the Holy Spirit. He was elected Vicar at the First General Chapter of the Congregation. Following the death of Father Félix de Jesús, he was nominated Superior General. He was born in Morelia, on December 20, 1900 and died in Mexico City on December 23, 1974.

(5) Agustín de Iturbide (1783-1824) was born in Morelia. He was proclaimed Emperor on May 18, 1822, and crowned on July 21. He was later fought by the Republican opposition and executed by firing squad in Padilla, Tamaulipas.

(6) Mother Guadalupe de la Mora, Theresian, sister of the Archbishop of Mexico (see previous letter).

(7) Ignacio Armida Cabrera, Conchita's son, and her daughter-in-law, Isabel Morán Bolaños Cacho.

(8) Jacobo Armida Morán.

(9) The four remaining siblings were Octaviano, herself, Father Primitivo, and Francisco Cabrera Arias.

(10) The twelve brothers and sisters, children of Octaviano Cabrera Lacavex and Clara Arias Rivera were: Manuel, Octaviano, Emilia, José, Luis, Juan, Concepción, Primitivo, Clara, Carlota, Constantino, and Francisco de Paula.

12

June 10, 1932

Veni Sancte!

My dear son Manuel:

I am very proud as a Christian mother, realizing how you long to imitate Jesus and find your happiness in following in His footsteps, suffering for Him! I am so happy! Combine divine prudence to your fervor; sometimes a holy condescendence pleases Jesus a great deal.

Did you finally go to Belgium? Obedience will always be God's voice, and souls are to be found all over the world, and so are crosses. What would we do on earth without crosses? Life would be unbearable without suffering, which unites, sanctifies, purifies, and obtains graces.

I am very grateful to the Theresian Sisters; they have always been so kind to me. I owe them many favors. If you are still in Oviedo, give Mother Mora my thanks. I told you in my previous letters that the Bank advised me about the 500 pesetas, that I wrote to the Post Office Administrator and he sent me your letter and they gave the money back. Lupe used it, as she is in need. She is expecting a little angel this month. Ask the Lord that she will be all right. She always has trouble. I always worry. Salvador is in bed with pneumonia; I also had this grief, but he is a bit better.

Chabela's children: Manuel, Carlos, Conchita — and it won't be long before Nacho catches it — have severe cases of measles. Yesterday Manuel had blood in his stool. He even had to be injected with serum, and we are afraid that Jacobito, who is only two months old, might catch it. You can see we are not lacking sick people and illnesses.

The boys are struggling, working frantically, and the inflation of the dollar has resulted in a loss of sales. I'm afraid they will have to liquidate the business or declare bankruptcy which Pancho says is a just death; in the end Ignacio, Salvador, Carlos, all of them, will be without work and it is very difficult to start over again in this crisis. But the Lord will not fail us. Pancho goes to Communion daily; pray the Lord they all keep their faith.

On the feast of the Sacred Heart, the Missionaries of the Holy Spirit inaugurated the "Casa de los sacerdotes" (1). It will take in the elderly who are finishing out their days, or who want to make the spiritual exercises or a retreat, or who need some rest; a very good thing for the Church. They already have helped many priests, though not in a special house.

I am sending this letter through the Theresian Sisters. I anxiously hope to know your whereabouts.

May the Lord fill you with blessings; do not forget this poor ruined Mexico, with communism at the top. God have mercy on us and may the Blessed Mother sustain our faith!

Your mother embraces and blesses you and asks you to pray intensely for her.

Concepción
(L.R., Vol. I/140-142)

(1) House for Priests founded by the Missionaries of the Holy Spirit as part of their apostolate on behalf of priests.

13

March 28, 1933

Veni Sancte!

My dear son Manuel:

I am not forgetting your birthday today, a happy day on which God sent into the world a new priest, another priest to give Him glory.

You are fortunate, chosen among thousands from all eternity to be another Jesus, to represent Him on earth and give Him many souls who love Him and adore Him! How sublime the mission of a priest! There is no higher dignity upon earth and in heaven; and all of them must be saints, representing the Saint of saints.

Listen: they say there is a book exclusively for priests entitled *Confidencias* (1). Have you heard of it? I will see if, through the Archbishop or the Apostolic Delegate, in which archdiocese it was published, I can get a hold of one for you.

I am writing to you in bed with the flu, but thanks be to God I am better and will get up tomorrow.

How many things have happened since you were born! How fast life passes, but it is we who pass. Everything we fail to do for others is smoke.

I am weak but will write again soon. What a queer manner of eating they have in that blessed land. It's only natural that one, who is accustomed to something different, be ill at ease. But everything offered up for Jesus is as nothing. Each country has its own customs.

I would like to visit Belgium, such a Catholic country! Here the Government ruled by masonry and communism is ruining us. Poor children! Poor parents who have this enormous problem of giving their children a Catholic education. Only God can save us! Poor Mexico! But the Blessed Virgin will sustain its faith.

I embrace and bless you with regards from all your brothers.

Your Mother,

Concepción
(L.R., Vol. I/154-155)

(1) This book contains some messages for priests. Leopoldo Ruíz y Flores, Archbishop of Morelia and Apostolic Delegate, gave it his Imprimatur on November 29, 1929. The publishing house, "La Cruz," later published four editions, the second one in 1961, the fourth one in 1974, the fifth one in 1991 and the sixth one in 1992. It is a private edition, exclusively for priests. Mrs. Armida does not tell her son about the real origin of this writing. She herself received these Confidences in Morelia during the years 1927, 1928, and 1929. At first they were given this title. Later editions were published under the title *To My Priests* (Archangel Crusade of Love, 1996).

14

April 26, 1933

Veni Sancte!

My dear son Manuel:

I received your letter and I am very sorry that you are suffering from arthritis. Drink three cups a day of a tea of boiled celery after meals. Try to eat a lot of celery in salad, eat the stems or boil them as I told you, it helps circulation. Also garlic is good for rheumatism. Take care of yourself; that is an obligation. The matter about your hand has nothing to do with this! That was not normal and God wanted you to suffer, but what is normal is that you take care of yourself. Look who is telling me to take care of myself. Let me know how you are doing.

They brought me to the side of the lake (1) for a few days of vacation. It made me sad to see that the house the Jesuits built for a Novitiate in this beautiful site has been expropriated by the Government. What a pity! All for God! I wrote to you during my spiritual exercises which were beautiful. Thank the Lord for me. The Sisters of the Cross (2) have a House here (3) and Sister Catalina (4) always remembers you and Father Carrera (5) in Gijón. She is a saint. From here I will spend a few days in León (6) to see Bishop Valverde (7) and the Sisters of the Cross (8) who have a house there also, and then, go on to Mexico City. Octaviano is 83 and says that if I do not visit him soon I will not see him. I hope the Lord will let me go and say good-bye to him, for the four of us who are still here are getting old.

Be a great saint. Pray for your brothers. I'll hear from you soon. Today I am writing only these few lines so that you will not worry about me.

Your mother embraces you and blesses you with all her soul and never forgets you and asks you to take care of yourself. Do not forget your brothers. A very holy Easter!

Concepción

(L.R., Vol. I/156-157)

(1) The beautiful Lake of Pátzcuaro in the State of Michoacán. In her *Spiritual Diary* she wrote: "I enjoyed the lake enormously, thinking about Him."

(2) The Sisters of the Cross of the Sacred Heart of Jesus had a House in that city. His Excellency Archbishop Leopoldo Ruíz y Flores asked for this foundation in 1912.

(3) In the city of Morelia, previously Valladolid. From 1925 until her death (which occurred in Mexico City on March 3, 1937), Archbishop Luis María Martínez was her spiritual director. He directed her spiritual exercises every year in this provincial and colonial city. The exercises of the year 1933 were the eighth he directed for her.

(4) Mother Catalina García, Sister of the Cross, former Superior, Vicar General, and Mistress of Postulants. She was part of the foundation in Gijón, Spain. She died on September 6, 1965, in the General House, in Coyoacán, Mexico City.

(5) Father Salustiano Carrera, S.J., who appreciated Mrs. Armida and the Works of the Cross.

(6) His Excellency Bishop Emeterio Valverde y Téllez, spiritual director of Mrs. Armida during the years 1904-05. Named Bishop of León, Guanajuato, he asked the Sisters of the Cross of the Sacred Heart of Jesus to found a house there. The founding took place on December 8, 1912. Mrs. Armida received it as a gift from the Lord on her birthday and Saint's day.

(7) Mrs. Armida sometimes stopped at the Sisters of the Cross House in León, during her return trip from Morelia to Mexico City.

15

June 6, 1933

Veni Sancte!

My dear son Manuel:

I got back to Mexico City, but am ill, and Lupe is taking care of Carlos and the children (1) who are also very bad. Carlitos, who is not yet a year old, might have surgery tomorrow because one of his ears burst. Please God he does not die on her; he is very weak. Carlos is without a steady job, only earning a commission on what he sells. Ask Our Lord to help him. Your brothers also are struggling and losing ground with the inflation of the dollar. You are lucky you do not have to deal with such worldly matters. Ask God to strengthen their faith.

The main reason for this letter is to congratulate you on your upcoming Saint's day; all I could offer up for you is as nothing, but united to Jesus' merits, it will help you immensely. It is said that Jesus complains because people see in Him the man and not the God-Man, the Divinity in Him, that if many priests would refrain from this way of thinking they would treat Him in a very different manner. His sacred Humanity is only a stairway, a door, a pathway to arrive at His Divinity, incarnate in Him. Think about Him in this way, adore Him, and die out of love for Him, for that Jesus God-Man to Whom we owe so much and to Whom we return so little.

I am writing to you from Lupe's house. I came to help her with her ill ones. First, I was playing the role of Mary in Morelia (2) and now the one of Martha. Blessed be God, because the most essential thing is to accomplish His will.

My dear son, strive to become a saint. On the Day of Pentecost, I had you on my mind most especially. Your brothers are going to write to you. Salvador is opening some agencies in the States.

Do not forget me with them, receive my blessing and send me yours. Your mother embraces you with all her heart.

Concepción
(L.R., Vol. I/160-161)

(1) Her children: Teresa Lafarga Armida first married Constantino Madero. They had two children: Teresa and Constantino. Following Constantino's death, she married a second time, to Jesús Mendívil Gil Lamadrid. Carlos Lafarga Armida married María de la Luz González Rojo Matute. They are parents of three children: Carlos, Francisco and María de la Luz.

(2) Where she had gone, as she did every year, for spiritual exercises, directed by Archbishop Luis María Martínez.

16

December 27, 1933

Veni Sancte!

My dear son Manuel:

Before this letter you will receive the death notice of Octa (1) (may he rest in peace). He died as a saint after fifty days of illness: first pneumonia and then a relapse followed by exhaustion, the kidneys, the heart, etc., also hives.

He longed for heaven and said he was anxious to go and see God; he was abandoned to God's will, but he did not want to get better. He suffered a great deal in the last years of his life. The wife of Jesús (2) asked for a divorce, and that's the way they stand before the law; so Joaquín (3) is very unhappy. Octaviano (4), what an ending! He lost 350,000 pesos on a farm they took away from him. The brewery at the point of bankruptcy, worse than ever, and he endured it like a saint. He founded a shelter (5) for poor girls and gave them 1,000 pesos each month; at the end he could not even afford this. Thus the Lord matured him for heaven.

They called me when he fell ill and I've been here since November 8th. I will soon return to Mexico City. He always asked me about you. All this has been a great grief for me, naturally speaking, because he was more than a brother to me; he helped the Works of the Cross (6) and he was a father to all of you when your father died. Blessed be God; let us adore His all-loving will! He is love and can only act out of love!

I received your letters and pictures. A million thanks. I am also grateful for my present of Masses! May God reward you! This house is finished. Everything passes away except what is suffered lovingly for God.

Primitivo arrived the night of the burial; he could not get here on time to see him although he hurried; he was on a mission in the State of Hidalgo. The night before last, Pancho (7), my brother, was praying at 8 o'clock when he suffered a stroke and fell flat on his face; they had to carry him, dead weight, to a bed. He gave us a good scare. Afterwards he went to his own home where he lives with Amparo (8), his wife, and Pancho, his married son with four children.

I'm catching the flu. I'll close until later. Do not forget your godfather. I was with him to help at his deathbed, and even up to the cemetery at Saucito (9) where our family has a chapel. Father Carrión (10), a Jesuit priest who died suddenly at home, is there. Luis Cabrera (11) is nearby at another school. I don't know if Bishop Martínez (12) was ever able to see you or will see you. Until next time, receive the blessing that your mother who never forgets you, sends you with all her heart.

Concepción
(L.R., Vol. I/168-169)

---

(1) Octaviano Cabrera y Arias, Concepción's brother and Manuel's Godfather. His wife, Carmen Hernández had died on December 23, 1927. His children were José Octaviano, Octaviano, Carmen, Mercedes, Joaquín, Luz and Jesús.

(2) Jesús Cabrera y Hernández was born in San Luis Potosí on June 3, 1893. He married Rebeca Sánchez, who died on October 29, 1918. He then married Guadalupe Gordoa Dumbar on August 28, 1924. They had three children, María Marta, María Teresa, and José Jesús Antonio.

(3) Joaquín Cabrera y Hernández was born in San Luis Potosí on September 22, 1886. He married successively two sisters, Guadalupe and Angela López Hermosa. Children of Guadalupe were, Joaquín, Guadalupe, and Clara. Angela was the mother of Octaviano, María de Lourdes, Concepción, Enrique, Salvador, and Manuel. She was also a true mother to her sister's children.

(4) Octaviano Cabrera y Arias, her brother.

(5) The Shelter "Gabriel Aguirre" in the city of San Luis Potosí, was actually founded by Dolores Manchichena, widow of Gabriel Aguirre, in remembrance of her husband. Octaviano was her executor and was in charge of the administration. Bishop Montes de Oca donated the land.

(6) The Works of the Cross are the Apostleship of the Cross, the Sisters of the Cross of the Sacred Heart of Jesus, the Covenant of Love with the Sacred Heart of Jesus, the Apostolic League (now the Fraternity of Christ the Priest), and the Missionaries of the Holy Spirit, for which the Lord chose as his instrument, the Venerable Servant of God Concepción Cabrera de Armida. Octaviano, her brother, helped all of them. On his farm named Jesús María, near San Luis Potosí, the first Cross of the Apostleship was erected. He also supported the Sisters and sent them vocations.

(7) Francisco de Paula Cabrera y Arias, another brother of Concepción, was married to Amparo Dávila. Their children were Francisco de Paula, Prisca, and Inocencia. The eldest, Francisco, married María Luisa Sancha and they were parents of six children: María Luisa, Amparo, Francisco de Paula, Clara, another Francisco de Paula (the first one died at one year of age), and Marta.

(8) Amparo Dávila, wife of Francisco, Concepción's brother.

(9) The cemetery of San Luis Potosí. Octaviano Cabrera y Lacavex was the first person buried there.

(10) Fr. Ricardo Carrión, S.J.

(11) Fr. Luis Cabrera Wilson, S.J., a son of Carlota Wilson y Urquidi and Luis Cabrera y Arias, the brother of Concepción who died while the Venerable Servant of God was on her trip to the Holy Land (see letters 58-59). The priest died on January 26, 1985.

(12) Luis María Martínez, Archbishop of Morelia, and later on, in 1939, Archbishop of Mexico City and Primate of Mexico.

17

March 3, 1934

Veni Sancte!

My dear son Manuel:

I wrote to you for your birthday and do not remember if after that; I am sure that one of my letters must have crossed one of yours. I was sorry Bishop Martínez was not able to go to Belgium. It was the Lord's will! He would have given you some good advice. Patience!

He was lucky to be in Bethlehem for Christmas. The Apostolic Delegate in Mexico summoned him to write about his trip, and he is going to publish it for him (1). I will send it to you. I mailed you a small book (it will be the last one of the author of *Before the Altar*) (2). As I told you, the title is *Jesus, What Is He Really Like?* (*Cómo es Jesús*) (3). A little grain of sand so that souls may come to know Him and love Him. I hope you like it. I would like you to make your meditation on it for a month's time. I want you to be filled with Jesus' kindness and for your confidence in Him to grow stronger. While I was writing it, I was often thinking about you. I wrote it as a present to Our Lord for the Centennial; ask Him to bless the book so it does good for souls, so they glorify God.

Here matters are worse, with ever more tyrannical laws. Everybody is complaining — about the schools, about the fact that one must pay one peso to every employee on the farms; agrarianism; the expropriation of religious houses and those that have been seminaries; the annexing of church buildings, temples; the prohibition of worship; finally Masonry in all its splendor wanting to copy

Russia, introducing communism by putting masons as teachers! Only God can save us! Our hope, after God, is in Our Lady of Guadalupe. You must have learned about the celebration in Rome (4), splendid, with the Pope, etc. Satan must be very angry.

Keep on praying for your brothers and sisters. Elisa with muscular rheumatism. María Cecilia, a girl of thirteen with a boyfriend that does not suit her. Pancho is being tested by Our Lord as Job, but remains firm in his faith. Ignacio does not receive Holy Communion often, with a big family, expenses and no resources. Salva (5) without children. Lupe suffering since Carlos does not have a steady job; as a salesman sometimes he earns something and at other times does not, living in poverty with two children.

Well, I will close now until later. Do not forget me in Holy Mass. Have a saintly Holy Week and a happy Easter. Your mother embraces you and blesses you, with my regards to everyone.

Concepción
(L.R., Vol. I/174-175)

(1) The book *A propósito de un viaje* (*With Regard to a Trip*) that Archbishop Martínez wrote under the direction of Archbishop Leopoldo Ruíz y Flores and was published by the publishing house, "La Cruz," third edition 1948.

(2) *Ante el Altar*, was the first book that Mrs. Armida published. She signed it with a pseudonym and, after that, she signed her other books: "By the author of *Before the Altar*." It has been reprinted a number of times and translated into several languages.

(3) This was her last book of meditations about Jesus, His mysteries, His virtues. She wrote it with the desire to present it as a gift to Jesus, on the nineteen hundredth anniversary of His Redemptive Incarnation.

(4) On December 12, while the religious persecution was unleashed in Mexico, a grandiose feast was celebrated in Rome to honor the Patronage of Our Lady of Guadalupe. Her image was placed in the Glory of Bernini. The Holy Father Pius XI assisted at the ceremony accompanied by cardinals and bishops.

(5) Her son Salvador.

18

April 19, 1934

Veni Sancte!

My dear son Manuel:

How have you been? I was ill last week with very high blood pressure, but they have already brought it down with injections, etc. It is about time for me to have something new since in a little over seventy-one years I have not had it bad. Whatever the Lord wills! We are His own, so may He accomplish His Holy Will upon us. Have you continued to take celery for your poor circulation? It would be good for you to take garlic: it is giving magnificent results. To 100 grams of alcohol, add a big clove of crushed garlic. You leave it out in the sun and also at night; after six to eight days you add thirty drops of it to water or tea, however you please.

Yesterday Father de la Maza was buried (1); a number of Jesuits have died here in a short time. I am very sad to see you always with such a troubled soul, hurling false accusations against yourself. When will you have peace of soul? When will you have faith and confidence? When will you really come to know Jesus and study *Jesus, What Is He Really Like?* (2), all kindness, mercy, pardon, tenderness, fineness, and LOVE.

Why do you think about yourself and not only about Him? You lack self-denial and confidence, you make yourself a child, rejoicing in your miseries; who does not have them? Consider that these are the only things we can call our own and that they attract Jesus: our lowliness, our nothingness. Miseries do not cause Jesus to withdraw from us, on the contrary, they are a channel we open for Him to pour in His mercy and His love. "Jesus is God's pardon." Who can be afraid? Occupy yourself in loving Him your own way, in the midst of your occupations, however you can do it, and He will be satisfied. Tell Him your desires, your interior and external wishes. I believe that you may aspire for another sort of work, ministry, etc. Ask Him for this, and if it is for your good, He will give it to you.

On Good Saturday, eleven Missionaries of the Holy Spirit were ordained: five here and six in Rome. A good little impetus for the Congregation. Thanks be to God! May they give Him great glory. Little by little everything gets done.

Here there is heartache especially over the matter of the schools: they want to impose Bolshevik schooling on the Theresian Sisters, they have taken away the houses of others and say they will continue to expropriate churches and the property of priests and religious! If God lets them! May He have mercy on poor Mexico!

A million thanks for the newspapers you sent me about the tragic death of the King (3). The whole world regrets it. What a difference a Catholic nation makes! All for the Lord.

They have done nothing yet to the Missionaries who have five Houses here: the Apostolic House, the House of Studies, the Novitiate, the House for Priests who want to make a retreat or rest, etc., and San Felipe, nor have they harmed the Sisters of the Cross. They say they want to tear down the Expiatory Temple, San Felipe. Do you remember it? It's right next door to San Francisco; the Missionaries are in charge of it and there they have perpetual adoration of the Blessed Sacrament and night Vigils with two or three thousand men. You can imagine how the devil must hate this! Our Lord have pity on us! You must have heard that they tore Santa Brígida's down to the foundations to widen the street. They say that they have let sixty thousand Jews come into the country and they already have several synagogues. Our Lord have pity on us all!

Imagine, María Cecilia, Pancho's daughter, is in love with a train engineer; she is only thirteen and is a boarder in Sacred Heart School, but she won't give him up and Pancho has even lost weight, he adores her so; pretend you didn't know anything about this, but pray for this intention. He wants to send her to Monterrey or to the United States, but, the money? Even so, he will make sacrifices. Young Pancho (4) is already seventeen, and is studying business administration. Poor boys in the midst of all of this! Ignacio with five, three who have died and another one on the way. Lupe with two: she's sick and having trouble. Teresita, the oldest, very bright for her age and very pretty, is nine. Only Salva has no children, pray to the Lord. Business seems to be picking up.

I will close now, blessing you and asking you for your priestly blessing. Your mother who never forgets you. Give my greetings to your Father Superior.

Concepción
(L.R., Vol. I/174-175)

(1) Fr. José de la Maza, S.J.
(2) She is talking about her book *Jesus, What Is He Really Like?* and recommends that he read it.
(3) King Albert I died in an Alpine accident on February 14, 1934.
(4) Her grandson, Francisco Armida y Baz.

19

May 30, 1934

Veni Sancte!

My dear son Manuel:

Tomorrow will be your saint's day, and I wrote to you the other day congratulating you and sending you my gift of nine complete days of my prayers and good works for your dear soul. I will have you present in my heart tomorrow more than ever, asking Our Lord to send you some very special blessings.

What you really need is to contemplate those horizons that seem new to you and to enter wholly into that world that seems so strange to you. You must put aside your ordinary meditation, that you cannot make now, and pray in a very simple and confident manner. What about getting in touch with Bishop Martínez, even if you do not choose him as your spiritual director? He is a saint, a holy man with a clear vision, and I am sure his spiritual counsel will help you, and your soul will find peace.

I have not sent you my spiritual exercises from last year (1), you will like them. Some short parts were printed with Bishop Martínez' permission, in the book *Jesus, What Is He Really Like?* Give it a try; you will not regret it.

I still have my ailments of the arteries and the heart. I am so sorry about your illness. Look in the drugstore for pure alcohol — not the kind for burning. Add 100 grams to a whole clove of peeled and crushed garlic and leave it day and night for four to six days, and then take 30 drops morning and afternoon in water. It will turn into a milky-like solution. Also celery is remarkable. I am sending you some Belgian francs that I hope will be useful to you; please do not be annoyed, and use them with the permission of your Superior. Until later. Peace, confidence and faith wrapped up in love; your mother blesses you and at the same time asks for your blessing and to not forget her in your prayers.

By the way, I was writing to you when the doctor arrived and he tells me that the best thing for your arthritis would be some of the baths over there (2) and that you take Vichy salt (3). All your brothers and sisters said they were going to write to you. Good-bye my dear son, I hope your health will improve and let me know how you are getting along.

Concepción
(L.R., Vol. I/178-179)

(1) Her spiritual exercises in 1933 had the theme of "Jesus' Comforts" ("Los descansos de Jesús"). Bishop Martínez directed them for her in Morelia.
(2) Medicinal baths for rheumatism and the salt waters for ailments used for cures in several parts of Europe: Biarritz, Vichy, etc.
(3) Salts from these baths. Also chemically manufactured, they have a curative effect on the bile and renal ducts, and indirectly, on rheumatism and various circulatory problems.

20

August 10, 1934

Veni Sancte!

My dear son Manuel:

Finally the Lord has permitted me to come to Morelia to make my spiritual exercises (1); I have been here for fifteen days now, I am still on retreat. I do the exercises without a fixed date, as long as He desires. I spend six to eight hours at the foot of the Tabernacle and we speak a lot. I have prayed for your dear soul and I guess you will soon be on your retreat if you are not already on it. I received your letter here yesterday, so I learned that you are in a retreat house suitable for taking a rest after the year's work, and that you will make your retreat before beginning the next school year. I will not forget you and hope you will not forget me either. I am doing these spiritual exercises to prepare myself for the "great journey," whatever God's will may be, but it is only natural at 72 to think about the next life seriously, the TRUE LIFE, the one that does not end and will make us eternally happy. Why be afraid of it? Jesus is "God's pardon." He wishes to save us even more than we ourselves wish to be saved and with His infinite merits we have enough and even a surplus to pay our debts.

Here worse days are coming with closed churches and a dwindling number of priests, only one for a hundred thousand souls, and thousands of unjust procedures. Masonry has demanded all of this, using all the leverage they have against the Church and against religious education. Pray for this poor Mexico that it will not lose its faith and that Our Lord will forgive us. It is time for my meditation, so I will end this letter sending you my loving maternal regards. May God make a saint of you, even if you do not feel it, by your always accomplishing His loving will. Your mother blesses you with all her soul.

Concepción
(L.R., Vol. I/186-187)

(1) The theme of these spiritual exercises was "Offer Up Jesus to Be Crucified" ("Dar a Jesús para ser crucificado"). She resisted this demand of the Heavenly Father, but finally accepted, and this doctrine was explained to her by her spiritual director and by Jesus Himself.

21

November 9, 1934

Veni Sancte!

My dear son Manuel:

I received your letter, which must have crossed mine, and the newspapers. Thank you ever so much. I will give them to Don Félix (1), because I do not understand them. Here, things grow worse every day; they keep throwing religious out of their convents. We are expecting uprisings and no telling what more. They already closed the Church of Santo Domingo (2) and they say they are going to reduce the number of priests even more; that the houses where a clandestine chapel is found will be expropriated without any further inquiry. Never has the religious persecution been so severe and drastic as now. Pray to the Lord for us. In the family there is no one employed by the government, except Angela (3), Luis' sister (4) who has to work out of necessity; she works in an office but expects to be terminated like many other girls for not having attended the anti-clerical rally.

Let us offer this up to God, that He may not allow this to continue much longer. What would we do without my Tabernacle? I would rather die. They say the Eucharistic Congress in Argentina was grandiose: from the President (5) down, they received Communion, thousands upon thousands of children and men! God be praised! Just imagine: yesterday I would have celebrated my fiftieth anniversary (6) if your father had lived. I am really old!

Manuel, how incorrigible you are! You agitate yourself and your soul, so loved by Jesus, that even He must resent this. Do you not have Him? If you have no virtues, you possess Him who has them all, and they are yours for so many reasons. Do not waste your time! Do not think about yourself, but only about Him. Make your meditation for a month's time with the book *Jesus, What Is He Really Like?*, and see if you don't acquire some confidence. We want to judge God according to our own thoughts, and we do not enjoy being miserable so that His infinite mercy may shine upon us. Delight in being nothing so that He may be everything, let Him be your Simon, and take up the Cross beside Him; if you suffer bitterness now, it is because He is saving up His consolations for the next life. Why be afraid of death inasmuch as it is the door to life? Discard those fears and misgivings. Everything that disturbs us and robs us of our peace of soul does not come from God. I never forget you and I will never forget you; trust the Lord, have faith and confidence and do not let yourself be deprived of peace.

All your brothers and sister send their regards, troubled about their business that is being destroyed by these disturbances, and about the education of their children. Your mother hugs you and blesses you.

Concepción
(L.R., Vol. I/193-194)

(1) Father Félix de Jesús Rougier, founder of the Missionaries of the Holy Spirit, was of French nationality. The newspapers her son Manuel sent to her from Belgium, where he had been exiled when the Jesuits were expelled from Spain, were in French and she did not understand it.

(2) The Church of Santo Domingo in Mexico City, cared for by the Dominican priests, is a beautiful colonial jewel in the ancient district of the City. There is a square in front of it with arches, where clerks help the public, and especially the students, type their papers. Nearby are the Faculties of Law and Medicine and the offices of the ancient University.

(3) Angela Cabrera y Wilson, daughter of Concepcion's brother Luis (see letters 58-59). She worked out of necessity in a government office. During those days all the employees were obliged to take part in the anti-clerical demonstrations. On the one hand, the Church prohibited this and, on the

other, the government fired those who did not attend. She died on December 15, 1984.

(4) Father Luis Cabrera y Wilson, a Jesuit priest, brother of Angela. Like her, he was a child of Luis Cabrera y Arias and Carlota Wilson y Urquidi. His father died while Mrs. Armida was on her trip to Holy Land and Rome (see letters 58-59). He himself died on January 16, 1985.

(5) Agustín Pedro Justo was the President of Argentina in 1934 when the Eucharistic Congress took place.

(6) Concepción Cabrera y Arias married Francisco Armida y García on November 8, 1884 in the Church of El Carmen in San Luis Potosí. Her recollection of anniversaries and memorable dates throughout the years is remarkable. The hundredth anniversary of their marriage was celebrated in the same church in San Luis Potosí, in Mexico City and in other cities all over Mexico.

22

June 9, 1935

Veni Sancte!

My dear son Manuel:

It was not possible for me to write before, so my congratulations would reach you for your saint's day. Forgive me, but I have been so busy with Lupe, and I am writing from her house. I wish with all my heart and soul many graces from heaven and I offer you nine days of EVERYTHING, for your beloved soul. Let Jesus and Mary congratulate you in my name and make you feel their love in which my own love is mingled like a little drop in the divine ocean. You shall see how in heaven your desolations on earth will be made up: Jesus is realizing HIS WORK in your soul: let yourself be MADE and UNMADE, unmade with a smile, loving your actual situation whatever it may be. Be faithful in spiritual dryness, in drought, in the Gethsemane of the soul, and "He who must come, will come." When? When He pleases to do so, but do not doubt His love, His preference for you among all your brothers, among thousands of souls. You have been a chosen soul for Jesus. I can testify to this; since your most tender years you loved Him, you preferred Him and longed to be His own.

Why be afraid? Do you still not know Him? Work to obtain self-denial and rejoice in your tribulations because these attract God's mercy upon us. He is so good! It is not the good things that God finds in souls which attract Him, it is He who puts in us the good He finds in our soul: don't let the magnitude of your misery keep you from contemplating the greatness of God's love, and resolutely concentrate on the graces He has given your soul. When souls look at themselves, they lose the time and attention to concentrate on God and His graces. TRUE HUMILITY is not amazed or frightened by what the Lord is doing in the soul because it knows that it is God Who is doing it, and it is not unusual for Him to do wonderful things, also because, knowing how secondary and worthless the soul's role is, it is not surprised when God pours His graces into it. When He is in need of a void, any void would be good. Try to live in a supernatural atmosphere, and never leave it; we must certainly see and touch this other inferior world, but let us do it as God does it, from the distance of eternity, without leaving His peace and His divine serenity. Live through faith, increase your confidence, your hope and throw yourself into the arms of love, in the Holy Spirit, to Whom I have prayed for you today, the day of Pentecost.

As I told you in my last letter, Lupe's operation was successful: they rearranged her bowels, removed her appendix, four times its normal size, and made room for her intestines (they could not shorten them because she might have died). We brought her back from the hospital and later that afternoon I went to the other French Hospital to see Carmen Armida (1), your aunt, and I was there at her side helping her at the time of her death; of the nine, she was the only member of your father's family left. Pray to God for her. I cannot let Lupe alone for although she is sitting up, she is still in pain and is unable to walk. I come to her house early in the morning — I am writing you from there — and I don't leave until nighttime. The Lord wills that I assume the role of Martha for now, but at least my health is not so bad. Pancho goes to Communion every eight days. Ignacio is the least fervent and in danger, not of losing his faith, but at least of growing tepid in the midst of the many people of every creed with whom he has to deal. Do not forget us; with all my soul and enormous motherly affection, I send you my blessing.

(L.R., Vol. I/214-216)

(1) The nine children of Ildefonso Armida y Verdejo and Petra García y Delgado were Rosario, Antonio, Ildefonso, Francisco, Dolores, Petra, Eugenio, José, and Carmen.

23

January 7, 1936

Veni Sancte!

My dear son Manuel:

I have no words nor sufficient heart to thank you for the 80 Masses you said for me and for my intentions! Only Our Lord can repay you for such a wonderful gift. May He be blessed a thousand times for having given me such a loving and good son. I was very much moved by your letter as were your brothers and sister: they are not as affectionate as you are, nor are they able to give me the greatest thing in heaven and earth, as you do. What a sublime thing it is to be a priest! What a wonderful predilection on the part of God to choose those souls for His intimate service and for them to continue His work upon the earth! Do not let a single day pass by without thanking Him for such a great favor. Among my seven children, you received the better part out of the pure goodness of Jesus who loved you so and who has given you so many proofs of His predilection. And you still doubt? Seek to love Him and make Him loved; think not about yourself but about Him and abandon yourself into His motherly arms, like a little child, because Jesus' heart is profoundly maternal. Is this not true? With Jesus and the Blessed Mary, what can you fear? Draw from that Heart your happiness, your peace, your food, your consolation, everything you need, light, grace, fire, recollection, love; live and die in Him, be inflamed and lose yourself in Him. Your confidence must be eternal, as eternal as is the mercy of God. I wrote to you in the middle of my exercises (1) from Morelia; did you not receive my letter? I talked to you a lot about spiritual things.

Pray to God for Lupe. She is quite ill with that atrophy of the intestines. Her liver does not function and she is in terrible pain. She appreciated your good wishes and sends her regards. Chabela (2) has an abscess from an injection and she has had to have an operation. Panchito (3) caught bronchial pneumonia in Saint Louis, Missouri that left him with fluid in his lungs. Pancho has gone there and must bring him back even though he has not finished the year and was doing so well in school. That will leave María Cecilia alone there — in the School of the Sacred Heart. You see how impossible it is with the schools here and their socialist education and text books. Nacho's children (4) are in small Catholic groups as they are able. Pray for the political, financial and religious situation here. Until later, I will say good-bye wishing you a VERY HOLY NEW YEAR; may Jesus fill you with His graces, His blessings, and with His comforts and caresses if this would be His pleasure.

Your mother who never forgets you, blesses you with all her soul. In my Missal I have your picture and am always praying for you.

By the way, the Apostolic Delegate will take Father Félix, I mean the Missionaries of the Holy Spirit (5), to open an Inter-Diocesan Seminary (6) in the United States for the Mexican Dioceses so the priests may be in a place where they will not be persecuted. There are many in Rome with Doctor's degrees from the Gregorian University. Next year there will be fifty-two priests in the Congregation. God continues to bless the work which is growing little by little. The Lord be blessed! Your mother blesses you again.

Concepción
(L.R., Vol. I/225-227)

(1) The spiritual exercises that she went to make in Morelia with Bishop Luis María Martínez this year were on the theme of the "mystical incarnation" ("encarnación mística"), the central grace of Mrs. Armida, a kind of spiritual espousal with characteristic traits of fruitfulness. The exercises

took place from October 13 to November 17, and are found in the 64th volume of her *Spiritual Diary*.

(2) Isabel Morán y Bolaños Cacho, wife of her son Ignacio.

(3) Francisco Armida y Baz, her grandson.

(4) The children of Ignacio Armida y Cabrera, her son: Manuel, Ignacio, Carlos, Concepción, Jacobo, and Isabel. The last two were still very small.

(5) A congregation especially dedicated to aid priests, promote priestly works and give spiritual direction to souls.

(6) This interdiocesan seminary operated for a time in Castroville, Texas. Later it was moved to Montezuma and was run by priests of the Society of Jesus.

24

January 28, 1936

Veni Sancte!

My dearest son Manuel:

Today is your birthday and I congratulate you in my own name and in the names of your brothers and sister. How very many graces of predilection has your soul, so loved by Jesus, received, chosen from among your brothers to the great dignity of the priesthood! Blessed be God!

Yesterday I received your letter dated on the 12th of this month and I am surprised that you have not received my letters. I wrote to you during my days of monthly retreat and two or three times more. The last one must have crossed mine. I spoke to you only about spiritual matters, I do hope you received it. My health is just so-so; you know, after 73 I cannot expect more. Jesus is our Master and He may do with His own anything He pleases. I am sending you a leaflet from the Covenant of Love (1) and another one of the Crusade of Victim Souls on Behalf of Homes (2); both of them pertain to the Works of the Cross or derive from them (3). I write them for the members. The Covenant has been established for many years now, and the Crusade is recent, to expiate and to obtain graces for families. You see how many divorces, adulteries, etc., need to be counteracted through the practice of virtue, love and labor, for the glory of God.

The Missionaries of the Holy Spirit are going to open an Interdiocesan Seminary in the United States under the guidance of the Apostolic Delegate, Archbishop Leopoldo Ruíz, because the Seminaries are persecuted here. They already have about fifty priests and others who studied in Rome and have a Doctor's degree from the Gregorian University who are going to be teachers there. Father Félix is so glad that they are bearing fruit for God's glory! This business of getting up at three o'clock in the morning might be harmful for you in the long run, it might be better to make your prayer at the same hour as your companions. Take care of yourself so you may give more glory to God. May the state of your soul be a continual belonging to Jesus, in this way, in a very intense intimacy with the Lord, expecting everything from Him. Thank you ever so much for the rich necklace of Masses you offered for me. Only Jesus can repay you for this treasure, already recorded in heaven. Thank you again a thousand times for such a marvelous and divine gift.

Pancho's health is not good, his kidneys, his mind — fatigue — so many cares overwhelm him. He was born for greater things, but has to live in the world and so many concerns preoccupy him. Panchillo is taller than I am. He caught pneumonia in the United States and had to be brought back; he is quite ill, pray to God for the health of both of them. Lupe is getting worse with her intestinal weakness, pray a lot for her and her marriage.... God be blessed! Ignacio with many debts and his family growing in number: his children (4) are with the Brothers of Christian Instruction (5).

Everyone sends their regards and I send thousands of blessings with all my soul and my motherly love. Become a saint and pray for me.

Concepción
(L.R., Vol. I/228-230)

---

(1) The Covenant of Love with the Sacred Heart of Jesus was founded on November 30, 1909. It gathers lay people who desire to live the spirituality of the Cross with greater perfection out in the world.

(2) The last work that she inspired: The Crusade of Victim Souls on Behalf of Homes, which hopes to obtain graces for the family. It was inaugurated

in Morelia on November 8, 1935. It lives the same spirituality of the Cross, but is not formally one of the works.

(3) The works of the Cross are five. They take in every category of Christian: lay people, religious, priests, bishops. They remind the world and help it live the gospel teaching regarding the fruitfulness of suffering when it is united to the saving sacrifice of Christ.

(4) His boys, Manuel, Ignacio and Carlos, of school age.

(5) During the religious persecution, the Brothers of Christian Instruction used to gather the children in small groups in private homes.

To Her Daughter, a Sister of the Cross, Concepción Armida y Cabrera (Religious name: Teresa de María Inmaculada)

In her *Autobiography*, Concepción Cabrera de Armida states:

"I wanted a little girl, and not so many boys, to offer up to the Lord, and right after Manuel, God gave her to me.

"She was born at daybreak in the same house as Manuel on Rosario Street, on September 29, 1890, when the bells were ringing for the Angelus.

"She was named María de la Concepción Micaela…. I was able to nurse her all the time it was necessary, thank God: she was her father's delight and both of us lavished her with blessings.

"Concha always had an angelic nature, a great purity and hidden virtues and qualities. Modesty was her characteristic. How many virtues I saw her practice in the intimacy of the family. The poor little thing suffered when she brought home the bill for school or when asking for something that she needed. She was a treasure, a pearl and not a shell (1), a lily that would be transplanted to Jesus' garden, leaving me because of His love. At fifteen she made a vow of virginity and at seventeen and a half, she entered the convent. Such a lovely jewel was not for the world, so the Lord chose her for Himself. Blessed be God forever! She was hardly able to talk when I taught her to say that when she grew up she would be a bride of Christ; playfully, I dressed her up as a nun and took her picture; I never said which order for I did not know any Sisters except those of the Sacred Heart. Who would have told me that later she would dress in a habit like those the Lord showed me, the habit of a religious order still to be born, but that already beat within my heart without my knowing it" (I, pp. 47-48).

She entered the Congregation of the Sisters of the Cross of the Sacred Heart of Jesus — inspired by her mother — at seventeen and a half, on April 17, 1908. She received the name of Teresa de María Inmaculada in honor of the Most Blessed Mary and because of her devotion to Thérèse of the Child Jesus, not yet beatified. She recited her religious vows on October 16, 1910. After this she was sent to form part of the Community of Puebla and later to that in Monterrey, where she caught Malta fever and sciatica. She died in the Mother House, 11 Mirto Street, on December 19, 1925, assisted by her mother with the special permission of the Archbishop of Mexico.

Her correspondence with her religious daughter was very plentiful and intimate. She spoke to her heart to heart, feeling fully understood by her. She presented to her daughter the ideal she herself would have liked to live, although she effectively lived it out spiritually throughout her own life. Volume III of her letters contains 189 letters to her daughter Concepción, in 238 pages. Volume IV contains 33 letters and other writings in its 239 pages. We have chosen twelve among them which we thought provided a good representation of a variety of occasions in the lives of both of them, starting with the farewell when Concha enters religious life, her reception of the religious habit, her religious profession; her periods of fervor, crisis, temptations, illnesses, her mother's trip to the Holy Land and Rome, congratulations on her saint's day, birthday, and Christmas, even when they both lived in Mexico City, on Mirto Street, or in Tlalpan. When she was sent to Puebla or Monterrey, she visited her several times. She used to write the customary monthly letter.

(1) Play on words: concha = shell.

25

J.H.S.
Farewell to My Daughter
On Her Entry into the Congregation

O Crux ave spes unica!

Mexico City, April 19, 1908

Concha, daughter of my soul (1):

With these lines your earthly mother wants to say good-bye to you as she gives you away to your mother, the Congregation, who through God's goodness, opens her arms to receive you on this day. You must be joyful about this exchange and thank the Lord with all your soul every day of your life. The first step you must give is to "forget the house of your father," to forget me…, all earthly affections, no matter how pure and holy they may be; so now you give yourself thoroughly to a single goal, to your only goal, GOD! With sacrifice, my dear daughter, all earthly loves are supernaturalized, made divine and are worn. So, from now on, this is the manner you must love, through God… in God… and for God.

Your gaze must be lifted very far above the earth, and even more so your heart, that heart which has cost me so many tears and sleepless nights… that soul which I endeavored to keep PURE, REMOVED FROM CREATED THINGS, VIRTUOUS, AND WITHOUT STAIN for the blessed hour I knew would finally come. Now, then, give yourself to Jesus, represented by your superiors; they are now your mother, obey them without hesitation, try to guess their smallest desires and confide in them, having a great clarity of conscience. They will always lead you to God; so let yourself be molded... polished... folded and unfolded... lifted up and cast down... kept and discarded... ALWAYS DOCILE, without any self-judgment, without voice or willfulness.

Obey! O and what a great virtue is this one of obedience! Without it you would not be a religious, even though you would have all the other virtues. Let poverty be your riches, let sacrifice be your life, suffering your ambition, and the cross your attraction. Self-denial, the stripping of your every desire, will be what you love most upon earth. And what shall I say to you about humility, Concha, pearl chosen by the Lord, to call you His own! What can I say?... Oh, that you might love it madly, with passion, and make your religious life, all of it, all of it, consist in abasing yourself..., in being always less..., in being unnoticed... in being despised, and loving all of this as the richest of all treasures.

To humble oneself is to be lifted up! ... To lower oneself is to reign!... It is necessary for you to deny yourself, if you want to pray well, to attract the gaze of the Lord upon your soul and to be a perfect Sister of the Cross, let your senses serve you only in the practice of this precious virtue.

Every day sacrifice one of them especially to your Jesus, and you will become accustomed to not living a moment without being a living holocaust, fulfilling your mission as a victim. I ask you to be always focused, my daughter: do not digress; curb your imagination. Live of the life of Jesus, of His charms and His beauty. From now on, you must lead an interior life, one of those that are so very intimate that the world cannot know, but one that your Jesus will provide for you, if you are faithful to Him.

Be faithful, correspond, daughter of my soul, to the very many, many graces of predilection in which you have been enveloped. Be faithful, extremely faithful to your Jesus, Who loves you so. Do not be deaf to His inspirations no matter how much it costs you to detach your heart from your "ego"…and from everything that can prevent your flight up to heaven. Consider that your true home is there, and you need to ascend by descending… leaving parts of your heart in the world. Prick yourself…renounce yourself…deprive yourself…crucify yourself! And what does all of this matter to a generous soul, to a heart on fire that is not detained by petty interests, but with ardor propels itself to love, for love's sake, Him Who is Love?

O yes, yes, Concha of my life! As I bid you farewell, I ask you, because of all the tears I have shed for you, to be generous… and not stingy with Him who gave His Blood for you, His life and His heartbeats, so you would be His… to purchase you the vocation to the Cross, with a love as great as His own heart, that has no measure in His mercies for you. Be a Saint Teresa in generosity and love your Master, your Treasure, your Heaven, your Jesus, with a seraphic love, a crucified love, a sacrificed love, with the love of your life's blood… with a love as immense as that of Saint Francis Xavier who said, "even if there would be no heaven I would still love You." God has given you a very big heart; do not waste its fire, which is so pure now, loving Him alone who is Love with all your strength. Concentrate there all your tenderness, your caresses and your sufferings! Do not look for consolation except in that divine Heart, for He will never deny it to you. Do not lose time with the straw of the world… in vanities that pass away… in colors that fade upon blooming. You were not born to fill yourself with smoke and trash, and THIS IS EVERYTHING THAT IS NOT GOD. Fly upwards… but how? By descending, always being the last, considering yourself unworthy of everything that surrounds you and finally realizing that "everything except hell, is good for you."

Be careful about being envious or jealous regarding real or imaginary preferences. Satan will use these to attack you: return his fire humbling yourself and taking pleasure in being considered the refuse of religion, for even if that should be true, it would still be an honor to serve Jesus in the most abject position, in the last place in the house.... Remember that high or low, in the arms or at the feet, religious life is a Cross and the sisters are the splinters which make it up.

In the midst of the natural sorrow of my motherly heart, I thrill with joy at seeing you form a part of the body of a Congregation whose soul is Jesus. I cannot explain what great things I feel when I see your belonging where my greatest love resides, in the "cloister in the form of a Cross" being a consolation to the loving Heart of Jesus. From whence do such things come to you? How very mysterious are the Lord's ways, and how incomprehensible His designs! I am able to perceive them in you and I am moved, and I cry and thank God with all my heart that something of mine, a piece of my heart, my blood, the beatings of my heart in you, is going to give some comfort, is gong to take away His thorns... is going to be a SPOUSE OF JESUS CRUCIFIED, CRUCIFYING HERSELF! O tender little flower, yesterday still mine! Go, fly to give your perfume to Him who created you for His own pleasure.

In purity did I receive you, and in purity do I return you to the arms of your Lord. Prepare yourself by that angelic virtue to be MORE THAN AN ANGEL... more than a piece of heaven... a spouse of the Lily of the valley, of the Brilliance of the Light Eternal... of the whiteness without blemish of the Immaculate and Holy Little Lamb! Be pure, daughter of my soul, completely pure in body and in soul, that a smooth crystal would appear stained next to your ermine heart. Purity... purity! It is the motto of this Congregation, but purity is only preserved in the hothouse of modesty and in the heat of sacrifice, so if you desire to be pure, you must be crucified, you must be a victim!!

And how are you going to achieve this? Through Mary, Queen of Virgins and of Martyrs, the Sorrowful Mother who obtained for you on her Feast the grace which you now enjoy. Let her be your star, your comfort, your teacher, your model, your fortitude, your loving mother who will cover you with her mantle... console you with her caresses... sustain you with her example, and who will espouse you, finally, to her Holy Son. In your temptations, look at her! Invite her into your joys... embrace her in your sufferings. She is Mother, and this designation encompasses the greatest that can exist, although it is not well understood! Walk hand in hand with her, rest on her lap, and she will console you... she will keep you warm; give you clothing, food, strength, counsel, life!

Study, and let yourself be formed with the milk of this Congregation for, if you are faithful, she will show you her treasures and will form you as a fragrant lily, as a precious living cross, where Jesus might have His delight, that Jesus, Who from now on, must be your dream, your life, your existence, your milieu, your all!! Slave and victim in union with the Divine Word, this is going to be your role. Happy you will be if you know how to play it well. AND ONLY OUT OF PURE LOVE! So, saying good-bye for always... upon leaving my rights over you as mother at the foot of the altar, in giving you to Jesus, to Mary, to Saint Joseph and to your superiors, I ask you on my knees to forgive me for my bad example, my weakness, unjust harshness and the many, many errors that I made in the education of your body and in the formation of your soul. Let others do for you all that I did not know how to do, cultivating you and making you flourish for heaven!

If I could, I would wholeheartedly give you not only one blessing, but a thousand; receive my blessing and that of your loving father who will undoubtedly do so from heaven; do not forget him in your prayers, and, my daughter, pray, pray a lot for all your brothers and sister. Remember practically your first words were to say that when you grew up you would be a "bride of Christ." You must know that the first time I took you in my arms when you were born, and when they brought you back when you were baptized, after making the sign of the cross upon your forehead and putting my lips on it, I offered you to Christ so you would be His own! I made you repeat this a thousand times when you were a little girl on the great feast days of the Church: and with the fire of my poor soul and through God's favor, above all, at home and in school, in the few pleasures and the many sorrows, I have been trying to conserve the same idea in your spirit, the sublime petition that the Lord deigned to hear... When you were 15 — do you remember? — the angels gladly heard that vow that the Lord inspired in you and that the voice of obedience accepted at the proper time: the vow of virginity! (2) The ups and downs of your life... the frenzied war of Satan, the impetuous winds of youth and imagination were not able to smother that flame, that fire preserved in the midst of many silly vanities.

Unforgettable things in 1907. My Lord! your poor mother, crossing through the heaven of your soul, saw the struggle between two spirits... tepidity, dryness, deceit and disappointments, tinsel that vanished, and with blood and tears, sufferings and torments, cried to heaven for your happiness, for your peace, for your vocation, for the happiness of what can be most loved in life, for you, my Concha of yesterday, for you, to whom seeming cold, I have loved so very much! So then, sacrificing to the Lord my great desire that you would be His own, I substituted my prayers, asking heaven to give you a husband on earth, alas! That He would make you happy on earth in the short term... but... suddenly the Lord came back to knock strongly upon your heart, and you answered, my daughter, daughter of my soul and He did the rest.

The hour came... He could wait no longer, and crucifying my

natural affections, the purest, most legitimate, and holy that can exist, He snatched you from my arms, ALTHOUGH WILLINGLY, and took you to those of another mother that deserves you, to prepare you there with divine love, to an indissoluble and eternal union! Jesus was jealous of your heart... He desired to call you COMPLETELY HIS... He wanted you to be His spouse. Can you understand what this means?

Make yourself worthy, through your simplicity, purity, humility, self-denial, and love, of such an eminent grace. Become a saint, my daughter, and good-bye until heaven! Forget me.... YOU MUST FORGET ME, and I ask you this with all my heart: I only beg for a memento, a prayer for her who was your mother, when you are before the Tabernacle. Let the Holy Spirit, font of all purity, communicate it to you through the cross, and keep your body and your soul always pure without blemish! Amen.

Your motto will be, from now on, Always pure and always victim! (Written at midnight to give to my daughter on the day of her entry to religious life, at seventeen years, six months, and nine days of age.) Mexico City, April 17, 1908.

(L.R., Vol. IV/19-27)

(1) In this touching letter Concepción reveals to us her tender motherly affection for her daughter, and we also realize the triumph of a superior love which leads her daughter to religious life generously, although not without pain, to the Congregation of which she herself had been the inspiration. This love is revealed in her counsel as a spiritual mother, as a mother twice over to her daughter, and her happiness in the midst of her suffering from this separation.

(2) On September 18, 1905, along with her daughter Concha and Fr. Maximino Ruíz, she spent some days at the Hacienda "La Cañada," belonging to her friend Mrs. Cerdán. These thoughts are found in some of the most beautiful pages of her *Spiritual Diary*. At the foot of an apple tree, her spiritual director read to them the Life of St. Teresa of Avila. On September 29 Concha celebrated her fifteenth birthday and pronounced a temporary vow of chastity in the chapel of the Hacienda. This is what Concepción is remembering. (*Spiritual Diary* 21/335-371.)

26

October 16, 1909

O Crux ave spes unica!

O, my Teresa de María (1), of Mary most pure! What can I say? What is it that my soul desires to say on this day of blessed remembrances for our hearts? What can the mother of a Religious Sister say, but to weep with her at the Lord's feet overwhelmed by the greatest and most immense gratitude? You were consecrated to Mary on the day of her Purity, a day that must make her smile amidst the choirs of angels, she, the Queen of them all. And you, too, my daughter, united to them must remember Her and receive that smile of your true Mother in the DEPTHS of your heart! It seems to me that she looks upon you, and this queenly Virgin also smiles at you seeing that you have been faithful to Jesus, that you have completed a year of wearing the royal habit of her divine Son, the Cross! That Cross which was His torment and His triumph, His martyrdom and His crown, that cross cherished by the Mother and by the Son, and that has been granted to you through a very special predilection.

Ah, daughter of my soul, a year has slipped by in the House of the Lord, serving Him and allowing yourself to be molded in the likeness of the lilies! Never feel regret but rather, with a still stronger eagerness, with an ever increasing ardor, continue your life of voluntary crucifixion without setting limits, either in martyrdom or in love.

Be always pure: because it was not by chance that you received the habit on the Day of the Purity of your Lady, of your Mother, and after Jesus, of your everything upon earth. Imitate her virtues, you who were my Concha, my jewel case for Jesus, the Pearl. Be a daughter worthy of that Mother of Purity and ask her to brighten you, to crystallize you, to purify you more and more to await the day, the happy moment when, with your lips, and even moreso your heart, will pronounce a name... that of the Spouse of Virgins! What an instant that will be when the whole of heaven will thrill in admiration, looking upon the greatness of a mortal creature!

O Teresa de María and no longer mine, or more mine, I will say with emotion! Do not lose time, for a single moment is precious in preparing yourself for the great day of your marriage to Jesus. Make Mary the Directress of your soul, and ask her to teach you how to be humble, obedient, self-denied, charitable, sacrificed. Ask her to make you love suffering and to understand the treasures it hides and that the world does not realize, but that a Sister of the Cross must study and embrace with holy enthusiasm.

Look, my daughter, and plan to always practice some virtue: if you are recollected, and you must be, this will be easier and even necessary. Never see evil in others and always in yourself. If you want to correct a Sister's defect, practice the contrary virtue, solely under the gaze of Jesus. Acquire an evenness OF SPIRIT. Never hold back out of human respect but run valiantly and generously to encounter suffering, no matter what form. See to it that since you are twice a daughter you must be doubly holy, humble and mortified. How very charming, my little daughter transformed into a true Cross, into an Oasis for precious Jesus!

O my Teresa! Fall in love to the point of madness, even frenzy, with this bloodstained Lily, this Lily of the eternal valley. Ask Mary to teach you to communicate with Him, to caress Him, to dream about Him, to imitate Him. Let Jesus be your only occupation, your thought, your life, your very existence! Do not think about yourself except to despise yourself, to humble yourself, to disappear and let others appear.

I close, then, asking you not to forget your poor earthly mother before the Tabernacle; only there do I want you to remember me, ONLY THERE. You know well my inadequacies and failures; you also know how greatly I desire the Lord's glory and the extension of His kingdom through the Works of the Cross. Pray for them and that God may be glorified and souls saved. Enter into the "Chain" and sacrifice yourself smiling, without knowing for what or for whom; this is the sublime mission, filled with charity and love, of a daughter of the Cross.

Your humble mother who blesses you.

Concepción
(L.R., Vol. III/12-14)

(1) Concha (Teresa de María Inmaculada) entered the congregation of the Sisters of the Cross on April 17, 1908 (*Spiritual Diary* 29/337). She received the religious habit and her name in religious life on October 18 of the same year. On that occasion her mother wrote a "paper" on purity (*Spiritual Diary* 31/123). This letter was penned a year after her daughter's reception of the habit, at the midpoint of her Novitiate. In it she reveals her maternal care and watchfulness as one who is twice a mother. How she follows her on her way, encourages her, and gives advice for her religious life, are truly noteworthy.

27

1909

Concha, my daughter, most beloved in the Lord: (1)

It makes me laugh to see that Satan has tried to catch you through affection and loneliness, etc.! All this must not bewilder you, and do not let it upset you! Temptations are ATTEMPTS of Satan, but a brave soul rejects them and gets rid of them, triumphing over him. I'll give you some advice, do not put too much importance on these temptations, or on many others that will come, either from love or from boredom with the Sisters. Do not fight them head on or try to overcome them with cloak and dagger, but rather let them alone, sidestep them, and... goodnight. I wouldn't hear of it — that affection for a creature, I repeat, can separate you from the love of the Creator.

Detach yourself from creatures and become accustomed to seeing in Jesus the love for your father, your mother and any other kind of love that could exist. He is your Father and more than your mother, the Only One Who can fill all the infinite depths of your soul. The Lord has given you that heart of fire to claim it all for Himself. How much the Lord loves you, and how jealous He is of whatever belongs to Him! Treat, then, with disdain those temptations and don't make anything of them: whether I feel them or not, if I cry, if I suffer, etc. Be valiant and strong, no womanly childishness. You were not born for womanly affectations, but to take on a thousand worlds, even martyrdom, if necessary, if they should impede your vocation.

Why foresee things that you do not even know will ever happen! You are already worrying about Tlalpan (2) etc., etc. LIVE

DAY BY DAY... then, whatever the Lord wills; abandon yourself entirely to His will. Especially in your case, for knowing how small and weak you are, the Lord always gives you things in small doses. I will go to Tlalpan if I can and the Holy Spirit will give you the necessary strength and even more: what weak faith you have! Lift up your heart and do not think about anything except to correspond to the eminent grace of your vocation, by being GENEROUS and by filling up the voids in your life with your humility, obedience, and fervor, and the DELAYS that you so guiltily gave to the Lord. And if I should die, what then? There is a heaven so great that we shall never be separated from each other. But no, I am not yet ready; though I am better, I am still weak. I hope that Gall (3) will let me to go to Mass on Thursday, but he may not because of the bad weather. God is thrice Holy and a THOUSAND TIMES MOTHER: what more can you desire? Onward, onward, and with your gaze fixed not upon yourself, but on Him, on Him alone, and acting only out of PURE LOVE.

Your mother, who wishes you to be a perfect Sister of the Cross, a copy of her divine Model crucified for love's sake, sends you a double blessing.

(L.R., Vol. III/15-16)

(1) In this letter, the Venerable Servant of God very prudently counsels her religious daughter who suffers temptations because of her emotional sensitivity. With a very acute psychological intuition, she teaches her that it is better to brush aside the temptations rather than fight them outright.

(2) The transfer of the Novitiate of the Sisters of the Cross of the Sacred Heart of Jesus took place during the year 1909. Sister Teresa de María Inmaculada is already worried about being separated from her mother, who lives at 3 Mirto Street, next door to the Sisters, whose convent is situated at number 11 of the same street in Colonia Santa María.

(3) Doctor Manuel Gallegos, widower of her sister Clara and her family doctor. In the context of this letter, we understand that she is ill and her daughter Teresa is worried about her health.

28

April or May 1909

My dearest daughter:

Do not be surprised at your spirit's state, it is only natural that after a period of fervor you experience some disturbances, but do not pay attention to them. Obey, close your eyes, and hold the Cross tightly; the one who obeys will obtain victory. Spiritual life is made up of desolations and consolations, and Saint Ignatius says that the right thing to do during desolation is to make no changes, and in a time of consolation not to cling too steadfastly to it, but to strengthen yourself for the next period of desolation.

Do not fear; these are clouds that must cross the sky of your soul, they are hurricanes that test the roots of the trees; it is summer and summers are harsh, dry, unpleasant and arid, but happy is the one who goes through them embracing the cross and letting Jesus ripen the fruit of the tree in His Heart. How would it be possible for your crucified Spouse to draw His portrait with a brush and lemonade? The One who is bloodstained must be drawn with blood and the Crucified with the cross.

Let yourself be molded, let the tempest rage without disturbing you, let the temptation pass and it will PASS AWAY, do not doubt it, leaving merits in your soul. And about Tlalpan! (1) Today it is this temptation, and tomorrow there will be another one. Close your eyes and let the Lord accomplish His will: take each day as it comes, and move ahead. Do not see enemies everywhere, so that if and when they should arrive, the Lord will have softened them up for you. Do not lose time as Satan wants, but offer everything up for the good of the Works of the Cross (2).

I am suffering from heart trouble: let it be as the Lord wills, but how can we not suffer at this time when the Works of the Cross (3) are spreading and vocations are flowering. I am very busy with priests and bishops (4); pray for me and forget all this nonsense. Ask the Lord that, if it is His will, I may die with a habit and religious vows, although I am far from deserving it (5). I will give your note to Pancho. Later on you will not want to leave Tlalpan (6). O my silly Teresa! The Lord trying to mold you and you are doing the opposite, how funny! No more of this: have a generous spirit, reject temptations, and do not drown in a glass of water, because you will still have to go through much bigger things smiling.

Your mother twice over blesses you and hopes you have a wonderful month of May.

Cruz de Jesús (7).

(L.R., Vol. IV/33-34)

(1) The transfer of the Novitiate to Tlalpan was being planned (see previous letter).

(2) Bishop Ibarra and other Mexican bishops were in Rome working on the permits for the Works of the Cross, particularly of the Missionaries of the Holy Spirit.

(3) For the foundation of the latter, and to obtain permission for Fr. Félix Rougier for the projected Institute.

(4) Currently, Fathers Soler, Ipiña, Daydí, and Mayer were studying the spirit of Mrs. Armida, at the request of Archbishop Ibarra and of José Mora y Del Río, Archbishop of Mexico.

(5) Her most cherished desire was to become a Religious of the Cross.

(6) Once she is in the Novitiate, she will be sad to leave it.

(7) Jesus asked Conchita to add the word Cross to her name (*Spiritual Diary* 1/174; 1894). She signed herself Cross of Jesus several times, and that became her epitaph in the crypt of the Religious of the Cross. Later her remains were exhumed and transported to the Crypt of the House of San José de Altillo, of the Missionaries of the Holy Spirit (1700 Universidad Ave., Coyoacán, Mexico City), where they are now preserved.

29

October 15, 1910

O Crux ave spes unica!

Teresa de María:

Today (1) I did not forget you, but no, this is not well-said, because I never forget you before the Lord: but especially today I placed you in Jesus' Heart, so that He will set you to burning with His celestial fire. Pray today to your holy Patroness to give you the ardent love by which she was set afire, as with love difficult things become easy, with love high mountains are climbed and surpassed and thorns are stepped on with a smile. With love nothing is hard, nor heavy, nor bitter, but delightful, smooth, savory. O love! If only we knew how to love, we would have everything! Ask for that love that consumes all earthly things in the soul, that lifts it up from the earth, that grasps man away from himself and propels him to every Calvary. Mount Calvary is the rendezvous for all lovers and there the Sisters of the Cross should be first in line.

Let all the Sisters surpass you in every other thing, but not in love, in humility, and in suffering. I ask the Lord for these three pearls for your spousal crown (2), how beautiful will your soul be in God's sight with these flowers that do not wither! Do not believe Sister Carmen's (3) death was just by chance; it was one more lesson the Lord wanted to give you so you could realize how ephemeral earthly things are. Do not be afraid that she will come for you soon: you still have to mature, to acquire a million degrees of graces and to help your Congregation. Prepare yourself peacefully and without constraint to be the spouse of the Crucified. O what a joy, what an honor, what an imponderable grace, that you will only appreciate adequately in heaven!

I am sending you some coffee cakes, almonds, and nuts, and a holy card or picture of Saint Thérèse, and your corset in case it might be useful (4). I send a letter from Manuel. Elisa wrote congratulating you on your birthday. I could not go to the funeral (5), nor to see you, today because I have been ill. Alberto and Gallegos (6) have already prescribed some medicines so that I can be well enough on the 23rd (7) to receive my Son-in-law. Tell the Superiors I will try to come tomorrow or Monday, and I send you the blessing of your mother upon earth.

Concepción
(L.R., Vol. III/23-24)

(1) On that day, she was celebrating her religious name day. She chose the name Teresa because she loved Thérèse of Lisieux, although she was not yet canonized. Mrs. Armida had a great devotion to Saint Teresa of Avila. During the days they spent at La Cañada, Father Maximino Ruíz read the Life of Saint Teresa. She must be remembering this (see letter 25).

(2) On October 23, she makes her first vows in the Novitiate of Tlalpan. Mrs. Armida writes in her diary (*Spiritual Diary* 34/333) "A happy day! O my Lord! From the time I woke up during the night, I have prostrated myself in thanksgiving for the priceless gift of this day."

(3) Sister Carmen Orozco, a novice of nine months, took her religious vows on her deathbed. Sister Teresa was a great friend of hers.

(4) These small gifts show us her delicate and provident motherly love for her daughter.

(5) The funeral of Sister Carmen Orozco.

(6) Doctors Manuel Gallegos, widower of her sister Clara, and Alberto López Hermosa.

(7) On that day, Sister Teresa will take her first religious vows as Teresa de María Inmaculada in the Novitiate of Tlalpan. Mrs. Armida and her children attended. Ramón Ibarra y González, Archbishop of Puebla, Father of the Works of the Cross, accepted her profession of vows.

30

December 25, 1912

Teresa, my dearly loved daughter in Jesus, in Mary, in Joseph, and in all the Saints that exist and are yet to come (1):

Yesterday I only sent you a few lines; it was such a full day with no breathing space, a torrent of things: the street, the tree, buñuelos, gifts, a poor child, writing, a simple "posada," I was just not able to get any rest until evening, and I went to throw myself dog tired at the feet of the Lord to await the Jewel of midnight. Didn't that Star of first magnitude fall over there? O what a lovely little Child! He made me cry, and you know that it takes cannon fire to make me cry. He is here! He is here!

What a great joy! He has made a heaven out of earth, and paradise out of a manger. Now the angels are coming to look for Him on earth, they had not been told where; now Villarreal (2) is full of glory, its silence is full of songs, and handkerchiefs are full of tears… with Him everything is pure, elegant, delightful, loving, immaculate, delectable; rich and full of light. Did she say no? Is it not true that since last night that Jewel has gone from arm to arm, from heart to heart? Be careful and do not leave Him alone, for He is so tiny and needs warmth, and tenderness, and caresses and care; do not let Him cry, because in this house (3) only smiles are permitted, tell Him, therefore, to take care not to be sad. Oh, what a handsome Spouse of the soul, full of elegance and splendor. He arranged it through a thousand means not to be born in his own home, but on the ground, like the worms, O my God! Setting His heavenly head on the earth, very close to the ground, like the animals. Oh, what a Jesus, Jesus, precious little Jesus, what kind of lessons are these? Let us not act like fools, my Concha, and let us abase ourselves… always grounded in self-knowledge, for from there we cannot tumble. Did she learn the lesson?

Well, now, I am going to talk to you about Mirto 3. There were the posadas: (4) and as we are six living here with Coronación (5) we had to make friends of the bird, the cat and the Pekinese (6). The bird, with such a nice song, started to sing, noticing that it was his posada! The poor cat wanted to run away; it was alarmed by the rattles and the racket of the boys. Only the Pekinese, accustomed to the rosary since he assists at it daily, was happy in the middle of the gathering; these were the first three, nuts costing next to nothing and empty boxes worth a penny. The servants were present and I played [the piano], a very simple thing. Yesterday the tree was pretty with small candles and we dressed an infant; it turned their stomachs to kiss him, but they did it. Memo came with Nacho and I kissed him, I held him, so he couldn't do anything. He was not ugly, at eight days old, with his little pillow and everything (7).

I am in a hurry and tomorrow I am going to clean the Mirto, so that Elisa can come (8) and see all her family, they will surely be eager to see her, and I also have to clean her place.… I found a house for them, it is the one where some Germans lived, on Fresno Street (9), do you remember? But the furniture has not yet arrived; I will prepare the kitchen and kitchenware that she will need, (10) and the dining room. Ask the Lord that I may behave well as a mother-IN-LAW; the whole thing frightens me. You are so fortunate that you are only the spouse of the King without so much ado and responsibility.

Pancho wants me to go with Mrs. Berta (11) to Veracruz to meet them; I will only go as far as Apizaco, because of the expense, just to make her happy. I am worried because they say a dog with rabies bit the Pekinese and they want me to kill him, but I have no heart to do so; also, I do not believe it, it was a man that he barks at because of his crutches; we will tie him up and see what happens and so if I catch the illness you will know where it came from.

My regards to Mother Javiera (12), tell her I will write her soon; give my Christmas greetings to everyone there in my name, to Asunción (13) especially; we are good friends. I went to Tlalpan, everyone sends their regards, and the Mistress of Novices (14) told me that you had written to her; become a saint, but of full stature, and not one of those "santitas" who hardly get off the ground, as Fr. Coloma (15) says.

If Bishop Ibarra visits there, tell him many things from me, and your mother blesses you with all her soul.

Concepción
(L.R., Vol. III/46-47)

(1) In this letter Mrs. Armida expresses herself with a great and charming simplicity. She naively relates to her religious daughter her preparations for Christmas and gives us a glimpse into the intimate joy of this Feast, that was very special for her, particularly after 1906.

(2) Name of the street where the House of the Cross was in Puebla. Afterwards, it was located at 5 South 1105.

(3) The convent of the Sisters of the Cross was familiarly called Oasis because it was to be a place of comfort for Jesus.

(4) The novena for Christmas, that was celebrated both religiously and in the family.

(5) The six inhabitants of the house are Mrs. Armida, her children Ignacio, Pablo, Salvador, and Lupe and her niece Coronación Cabrera Sotomayor, daughter of her brother Juan, and who lived in her house.

(6) A Pekinese dog.

(7) For Christmas she was accustomed to sew clothes for a poor child. She called someone, dressed him up, and asked her children to kiss him.

(8) Her daughter-in-law Elisa Baz y Duclaud, married to her son Francisco Armida Cabrera on August 2; they were returning from their honeymoon.

(9) A street in Colonia Santa María, near to that of Mirto.

(10) Earthen vessels for cooking, common in Mexico. She uses this expression in a general and familiar way to designate kitchen pots and pans.

(11) Mrs. Bertha Duclaud de Baz, mother-in-law of Francisco.

(12) Mother Javiera Perochena who had been Superior General of the Sisters of the Cross of the Sacred Heart of Jesus. She was elected on November 4, 1921. At this time she lived in Tlalpan.

(13) Mother Asunción Marín, Sister of the Cross of the Sacred Heart of Jesus.

(14) Mother Concepción García González, Mistress of Novices.

(15) Father Luis Coloma, a Jesuit priest, author of several books for young people. He sought to instruct them, reinforce their morals, as well as entertain them.

31

1912

Teresa de María (1):

What a shame that she is ill! My dear daughter wanted to be the first one to try out the infirmary quarters: they are so charming.

How are you getting along? Let yourself be cured without saying no to anything except to your own judgment and will. What a gold mine illnesses are if they are well suffered for God's sake! He now wants to give you the crown of patience; do not reject it so that it will become such a big crown that it will fall off your brow. Don't you see by now the results of becoming irritated? and over what! Oh my God! And what a waste of time to be thinking about creatures and filling oneself up with silly thoughts... "what if they don't love me any more, what if they don't pay any attention to me, what if I bore them, what if I no longer please them...."

God help me! Why lose yourself among created things? Teresa, look for a Good that encompasses all that lives. You are flesh and are looking for the spirit? Let go of the flesh and you will find the spirit. This is what is missing, my little elephant, (2) even though it is hard on you; it does not cost all that much if you don't give in to your imagination. Oh, that imagination, Teresa! it will be the death of you if you do not curb it on time, if you do not amputate it and put it under your feet! Look: no matter how many children there are, each one of them has his or her own place; they are not cast out of the heart to make room for the others; every kind of motherhood is derived from God, and for that reason has the gift of expanding itself. It is only natural that those who have newly arrived get the most attention; this is only normal, it's obvious that the little ones are held, and the older ones are put into walkers.

Oh, how silly of you, my dear Teresa! my little one, God keep you. Lift up your eyes and fly, my angel, to those other regions for which you were born. I am going to offer the sacrifice of not going to see you while you are ill until you are well. You see, my dear daughter, we are in a critical time during which the foundation of the masculine branch (3) is in the balance; offer your suffering for this intention and help me, in my dual role, to obtain this great grace from the Lord that men will not frustrate His will... dedicate yourself to this, with your communions and good works: that everything may be settled during this May or June. So now then, think about those golden horizons of the glory of God and of a similar future for our beloved Oasis. I am anxious to know how you are feeling; you know that my Angel of Purity (4) which is also yours, is near you in the heart of your humble mother.

Concepción
(L.R., Vol. III/48)

(1) In this motherly and very intimate letter, Mrs. Armida supports her religious daughter with great tact, helping her to overcome her excessive sensitivity and imagination. First, she expresses her concern for her illness, and afterward she sweetly and even laughingly reprimands her, so as to open more elevated horizons for her that will help her overcome her self-centeredness and turn her thoughts and energies to higher pursuits. Her practical psychology can be seen in use here.

(2) Mrs. Armida was tall and stout; sometimes she signed herself: "your mother elephant" and here she calls her daughter "my little elephant."

(3) At this time (1912) Bishop Ibarra and other Mexican bishops were laying the groundwork in Rome for the foundation of the Missionaries of the Holy Spirit, religious and priests who would form the fifth Work of the Cross. They were also asking the Superiors of the Society of Mary, to permit Father Félix Rougier of their congregation to return to Mexico for this purpose. Mrs. Armida prayed a great deal for this intention which was so close to her heart, and asks her daughter to interest herself generously in this matter. Called by his Superiors, Father Félix had left Mexico in 1904 and found himself in Spain, awaiting the permission of his Superiors, who represented God, to dedicate himself to this Work which he felt to be the will of God. His obedience during these ten years or so of "exile" may be called heroic.

(4) The Angel of Purity was the personal Angel of Mrs. Armida and of the Oasis. Fr. Félix brought back from France a beautiful engraving that represents it. The original is kept in the Mother House of the Sisters of the Cross of the Sacred Heart of Jesus, in Coyoacán, Mexico City. In the House of Jesús-María, San Luis Potosí is a painting of the Angel made by Fr. Guillermo Grave, M.Sp.S., which has been reproduced on holy cards.

32

September 16, 1913

O Crux ave spes unica!

My dear daughter Teresa:

Today, September 16, while resting here and taking advantage of being on land, I send you these lines, still seasick and believing, I could swear, that I am still moving. What a horrible thing this seasickness is! Since I boarded the boat on the 27th, I could not pray or read or see or hear, nausea and vomiting and an awful general upset; those who know say it was an uncomfortable trip, but a good one. We still have forty more hours by sea to Barcelona tomorrow, where we will rest for three days. I, of course, saw nothing in Havana or in New York.

Today I want to visit the Cathedral to visit the Blessed Sacrament for which I hunger, and to see the monstrance that has grapevines made of emeralds, and bunches of grapes made of pearls. With a great effort, I get up to receive Holy Communion, but no thanksgiving or anything. Always on deck, and not even then am I better off. God be praised! I'll be able to rest in Barcelona; from there I will go by train to Lourdes and up to Marseille where I board a ship to Jaffa. All of this is assuredly a small thing for the joy of seeing and kissing the Holy Land.

I have not forgotten you; you chose the better part, and never regret it. A young dancer came on board and we were able to arrange for her to make her First Communion on the 14th. Poor girl! She ran away from her mother and came all by herself from Italy; now she will go back repentant, the Lord has taken care of her. She is called Gioconda. We all gave her presents and she cried. She confessed twice to Bishop Ruíz (1).

So keep on praying for us to God, and I will write from Barcelona. It seems to me incredible to be going in this direction; I know my geography. What a huge sea the Atlantic is! Tomorrow we shall enter the Mediterranean. Good-bye and your mother blesses and embraces you and asks you to tell Mothers Ana (2) and Magdalena (3) that I will write to them another day, for I am out of breath. Everybody sends you regards and embraces you along with me.

Concepción
(L.R., Vol. III/49)

(1) The Archbishop of Puebla (Ramón Ibarra) organized a Mexican Pilgrimage to the Holy Land and to Rome to pray for Mexico. It seemed to him a great opportunity to bring Mrs. Armida to Rome in order to finish obtaining the permission necessary for the foundation of the Missionaries of the Holy Spirit. Bishop Maximino Ruíz, recently nominated for the Diocese of Chiapas, and Bishop Amador, were also on the trip. Her son Ignacio, then twenty years old, and her daughter Guadalupe, who was fifteen, accompanied Mrs. Armida.

(2) The Reverend Mother Ana de María Cabrera (Ana Apolonia Cabrera y Otahegui), third daughter of Don Florencio Cabrera y Lacavex and Manuela Otahegui; she was therefore a cousin to Mrs. Armida. She was born on August 25, 1862. She married Pedro Sousa but had no children. When she became a widow, she entered the Congregation of the Sisters of the Cross, inspired by her cousin. She was the first Superior General of the Institute.

(3) Mother Magdalena Campos, Sister of the Cross, by then Superior of the House of Puebla.

33

December 14, 1913

My dear Daughter Teresa:

Many thanks; I received your letter of congratulations today; I spent the day in Santa Maria Maggiore clearing out my accounts of 51 years with the Lord Jesus (1). I am bankrupt and you must help me. What a month I have had in Rome, I tell you! We settled everything on the 13th. I have so many things to relate. Nobody would ever have suspected such enmity toward the Works of the Cross (2). A terrible atmosphere against all of the Works, a predisposition by those in high places. Thanks to letters, the comings and goings of Bishop Ibarra (3) who was ill, the examination, etc., light began to emerge, albeit through much mortal suffering, trusting in God and preparing myself for a beating should God so will.

Between one thing and another, I visited church after church and the nuns... I went to the Gesú (4) where Saint Ignatius is and an enormous, beautiful silver statue: I usually go to Mass there, it is quite near to the Hotel which is just a short distance from Piazza Venezia. You would laugh if you heard me speak Italian! I just received an employee from the Vatican, he seems to be a real gentleman, with a letter for an audience for tomorrow (5) with seven other persons. They call me Conceta.

With priests and drivers and butlers I make myself understood. They think I am Argentinian; sometimes I say that I am a Spaniard, because when I say Mexican, they ask about the war. Molto bello, mattina, sera, questo giorno, caldo o freddo, andiamo presto, ecco, la signorina, il soldo o la lira. Chiesa Santa Lucia. Here everything is very sweet; men kiss each other (6). I was at the funeral of Cardinal Oreglia (7). Such lovely choirs! There were no musical instruments yet the Sistine Chapel seemed to have an orchestra.

I visited the crypt of Saint Peter; thirty-eight popes are buried there. There is a Virgin at whose face a ball was thrown, you can see the wound from which blood flowed, and she cures no matter what illness. I go about Rome by myself. Such churches, you have no idea: marbles, mosaics, paintings, caissoned ceilings. But what I like the most is that Jesus is the same in these royal thrones as in poor Mirto (8). He is in the midst of two or three thousand candles in fanciful forms; I would like to take some of them to the sacristans of the Cross (9).

I still do not know when we are leaving, perhaps on the 20th, for Assisi, Loreto, Florence, Luca, Venice, Padua, Milan, Lyon, Paray-le-Monial, and Paris. As an offering, Archbishop Ibarra is taking a very rich and beautiful golden heart with a Cross of the Apostleship (10). On it is engraved: "Forgive Mexico that consecrates itself to You, and give us your peace," and the names of the pilgrims are on cards on the inside; it opens as a reliquary.

Then to Lourdes and Manuel (11), Madrid, Avila, and Barcelona. I will go to see Thérèse (12), although I do not feel like doing anything. Pablo (13) is always in my heart, notwithstanding all this movement. Good-bye my little daughter, and become a saint. Your mother blesses you.

Concepción

How happy I am to know you are contented with Mother Grandmother (14). It could not be otherwise! Enjoy her and be worthy of such a Grandmother who loves you so.

Concepción
(L.R., Vol. III/65-66)

(1) Mrs. Armida was born on December 8, 1862, and had just celebrated her 51st birthday. She spent it in a spiritual retreat as was her custom.

(2) When they arrived in Rome, Bishop Maximino Ruíz encountered Archbishop Ibarra and Mrs. Armida. He had gone there beforehand and told them there was very bad news about matters regarding the Works of the Cross which they had come to finalize. Some false and calumnious information and false revelations had predisposed cardinals and bishops against them.

(3) Ramón Ibarra y González, Archbishop of Puebla, had arranged permission and indulgences for these Works, and he had now gone to Rome to ask expressly for the foundation of the Missionaries of the Holy Spirit and to ask that Father Félix take care of this enterprise. The Archbishop did not spare any effort or hardship, although he was ill and had an ulcer on his foot.

(4) The Gesú is the Church of the Jesuits in Rome.

(5) With His Holiness, Pope Pius X.

(6) Customary salutation in Europe.

(7) His Eminence Cardinal Luigi Oreglia di San Steffano, Camarlengo named a cardinal by His Holiness Pope Leo XIII.

(8) Her home, situated at 3 Mirto Street, where she had a Tabernacle, through indult of the Holy Father Pope Pius X.

(9) The Sisters of the Cross had their convent at 11 Mirto, on the same street as Mrs. Armida. The sacristan took good care of the Blessed Sacrament, solemnly exposed day and night for their adoration.

(10) The Cross of the Apostleship is the graphic expression of the message of the Works of the Cross, a big Cross with a living Heart in the center, crowned by the Holy Spirit. It encompasses the complete message of human salvation through Christ's sacrifice upon the Cross and the glory that this same sacrifice conferred on the Holy Trinity.

(11) Her son Manuel Armida y Cabrera, a Jesuit student, who was in Loyola and whom she has not seen for several years. Afterward, he made the sacrifice of not returning to his country.

(12) Saint Thérèse of the Child Jesus, to whom she had especially commended the foundation of the Missionaries of the Holy Spirit and permission for Fr. Félix to dedicate himself totally to them.

(13) Her son, Pablo Armida y Cabrera who had died on June 27th of the previous year from typhus. One is profoundly moved at the revelation of this great sorrow that even now deeply wounds the heart of the widowed mother.

(14) Mother Ana de María Cabrera (see letter 32). This spontaneous letter has the charm of her simplicity. She must have written it in a hurry. One can find almost no punctuation in the original.

34

September 29, 1915

Teresa de María, my dear daughter:

Today is your twenty-fifth birthday and from my retreat I send you my most heartfelt congratulations. I compliment you for NOT HAVING BEEN DEAF TO THE LORD'S CALL and for having consecrated yourself to Him from a very early age, first in La Cañada (1) and afterward in religious life. Blessed are you for having chosen the better part, or better yet, blessed be the Lord, Who chose you for Himself without your being worthy of it and took you away from the dangers and misfortunes of the world; Who cared for you as the apple of His eye and loves you with a finesse and tenderness you will never fully understand.

I am very happy to have a daughter who belongs completely to Jesus, it seems to me that you are a little lamp which burns constantly on my behalf; I believe that you and Manuel will take me up to heaven.

But let's take stock: how have you reciprocated the many benefits the Lord has bestowed on you from the time you were born, since you entered religious life? Have you been aware of the greatness of your vocation? What impediments stand in the way of what the Lord desires from you? The heart… the humanized affections, the imagination! I am going to give you some advice, you have entered the cloister of earth, but you have yet to ENTER THE CLOISTER OF THE HEART OF JESUS to lose yourself there, to drown yourself there, to burn, consume and sublimate yourself there, engulfed in the sweetness and sorrows of which it is full. In that loving heart, there are many dwelling places; ask the Blessed Virgin to choose a place for you and she will show you the way around this "Enclosed Garden" presenting you with the treasures that are hidden there. The gazes of the Father and the Holy Spirit take their delight there: it is a most precious garden whose image the Oasis must reproduce here on earth, the "Houses of the Cross." There you will listen to the divine inspirations more closely than anywhere else, and you will UNDER-STAND the language of the Cross....

But I do not want to deceive you; there you shall also experience much suffering, much bitterness, but in UNION with Jesus, Who sweetens everything, making you as worthy as possible, to enter into His secrets and His sorrows. There, within this Divine Heart, the soul is transformed from being earthly to being spiritual; there all vanities and human attachments are seen from afar. Enter there, my daughter, and never turn back. Lose yourself, I repeat, in the beauty and infinite perfections of Jesus — hidden, pure and self-sacrificed — accomplishing your mission to remove the thorns that crown the Heart of Love. Heaven needs victims, but in union with the Heart of Jesus. Jesus needs faithful souls into whom He can unload His pains and sorrows, and He does not find them....

The Congregation needs pure and self-forgetful souls, who are anxious only to console Him, to expiate for the millions of sins by which He is offended, to fashion a place of rest for Him. This Divine Heart is especially in need of love, love, souls ready to be consumed in the fire of the Holy Spirit. Teresa de María, do not soil your wings with the grime of human caresses! You were born for greater things, to love a Good that encompasses every good, beauty and delight. And this is Jesus who wishes to envelop you in the fire of His love.

Ask Him for a fire that will turn to ashes all earthly loves, vices, and defects of your soul. Ask Him for a powerful and active love, so unique that it shall attract you to Him as a magnet attracts iron, growing with every Communion, with every instant, consuming you in a martyrdom of love. Jesus has many kinds of victims, but FEW VICTIMS OF LOVE, says little Thérèse (3). O, if you were one of them! Ask of her to love Jesus with such impetuosity that your love would sweep away all the crosses and pains of life. Ask to love Him with a love that illuminates, vivifies and purifies everything; with a most faithful love in its unending, prompt, and generous correspondence to grace.

How I wish that you would burn with a passionate love, a love through which you would be attracted solely to the supreme object of your tenderness, to Jesus on the Cross… I would like to see your soul with a love so prodigiously expanded by sorrow, by the deceptions and deceits of the world and its creatures that it could be called a MARTYR'S LOVE, a sanctifying and most pure love. With the Holy Spirit Himself — His presence, face and company being familiar to you — love with that love which surpasses all created things. Lift high the aspirations of your soul, my dear daughter, fighting against your passions, BUT IN PEACE, nullifying your own will.

Everything for God, nothing for yourself, so that any crucible that would purify you would seem small. Lift up that heart of yours! Do not drown in so little water. Heaven is awaiting you pretty soon! "A LITTLE MORE." Say it every day, vehemently wishing to have the humiliations and contempt of the world, to be more like Jesus! "To the extent that the soul conforms itself to the spirit of Jesus, it walks in true sanctity." Everything else is an illusion.

So now, then, enter fully into the true Cloister of the Divine Heart where the authentic Religious dwell. But remember, it is said that no one is worthy to dwell in that divine place, except the one who dies to all self-love and the natural desires of this life. The Heart of Jesus is a place of REST, but only for those who mingle no other loves with this one, and are satisfied with this love alone. It is life, but only to the souls who, RENOUNCING THEMSELVES, have died to pride and vanity. And if Jesus permitted His side to be opened after His death, it was to show us that there is room there only for those who are CRUCIFIED AND DEAD TO EVERYTHING THAT IS NOT HE.

So now you know the way. Also consider that Jesus let His Heart be opened after He had suffered so much, to indicate to you that all sufferings and uprootings are costly, until the soul reaches that Heart, because there every bitterness is sweetened and all pains are soothed. If death was strong enough to separate His soul from His body, it was not able to stop His love, and from that moment, He thought about this House, He thought about His Teresa, and opening His holy chest, He formed inside of it a nest of love in which to hide you, a volcano of love to warm you. Quench your thirst for affection in that divine Fountain, and you will be satisfied, and you will be happy, and this is what your mother desires for you with all her heart as she blesses you.

PRAY FOR ME.

Concepción
(L.R., Vol. IV/47-71)

---

(1) A farm belonging to Mrs. Guadalupe Cerdán, near Mexico City, where they spent a vacation, and Concepción Armida Cabrera made her first vow of chastity (see letter 25 and note).
(2) Oasis is a symbolic name for the Houses of the Cross, for in them the Sacred Heart of Jesus is supposed to receive comfort in the midst of the world.
(3) Saint Thérèse of the Infant Jesus, at the time not yet beatified, very much loved by Sister Teresa de María Inmaculada. She chose her name in religious life out of her affection for this young Carmelite.

35

August 25, 1923

Teresa de María, my dear daughter:

Today I want to talk with you about Love; sanctity — Saint Thomas Aquinas says — (1) does not consist in knowing much, in meditating much, or in thinking much, but IN LOVING MUCH. Jesus is not loved! And you are called, by reason of your vocation, TO LOVE HIM IN THE PLACE OF THOUSANDS OF SOULS.... Imagine that every once in a while He asks you, "Teresa, do you love Me more than these?" And let us see what you answer Him; be careful not to remain silent. How these words of Jesus make one shiver on hearing them! And you must listen to them, striving always to grow in practical LOVE, in the sacrificial love that crucifies, in your love for the Eucharist and for souls. JESUS IS NOT LOVED! And you must make up with interest this OMISSION OF LOVE, LOVING and comforting His all-loving, all-sorrowful Heart, whose beats are nothing more than tenderness, forgiveness and mercy towards you.

But how can Jesus be comforted, how can one's own offenses and those of the materialistic and impure world be expiated? BY LOVING! You must be A SOUL ENAMORED OF LOVE, a victim of love, a chalice of love, a living host, the flour of this host, to contain Jesus, TO BE TRANSFORMED INTO JESUS! Hosts are pure, hosts are white, and I imagine them turned red within the Sacrifice, which although it is bloodless — without blood shedding — the blood of the soul, the holocaust consummated there, must be red. The Sisters of the Cross must be of snow and blood, pure and victim, living from sacrifice. This is the true love that assimilates one to Jesus.

To live of the Cross is to live of love! It is necessary to make a habit of looking at everything, great or small, as coming from the loving hand of God FOR YOU, rejoicing out of love in His Most Holy Will, although it may crucify you. You must ripen in the warmth of the divine Sun Who from the Cross asks you only to REMAIN UNDER HIS RAYS. "Teresa, my daughter," He seems to say to you, "Remain in my love." Tell Him frequently, "O divine Hand, work upon this nothingness who wants to love and remain in You!"

Be confident, because a lack of confidence is the WORST INGRATITUDE. If you have offended Him, it does not matter! He always loves you; BELIEVE IN HIS LOVE and do not fear. He is always anxious to forgive. O what a Jesus! If He allows temptations, it is to make us humble. What can prevent you from loving Him? He knows your misery more than anyone else and He loves you thus; our lack of confidence hurts Him, our FEARS wound Him. "What was Judas' disgrace?" Not his treason, nor his suicide, but "NOT HAVING BE-LIEVED IN THE LOVE OF JESUS." Jesus is GOD'S PARDON. So then, love Him day and night and always, with each beat of your heart, so that He will smile upon you and give you the blessings of His love. I suffer when souls make a Nero out of Jesus. Not so with you, my daughter, I hope that He may never find in you the coldness of mistrust and ingratitude.

Ask Him that you may love Him much, and make Him loved, pray that He will set the hearts of the Oasis, of priests, afire with His own Heart, a volcano of love; that He will inflame them and melt them so that they will preach a LOVING Jesus, so as to obtain a LOVED Jesus, because one always obtains results when one BELIEVES IN HIS LOVE. But no good can be done WITHOUT IMMOLATING ONESELF; pray that priests may LOVE THE CROSS: the fruitful apostolate is the one undertaken knowing how to sacrifice, labor and struggle to make LOVE LOVED. The priest who LOVES will never be defeated.

You also, because of your vocation, must be like a priest, offering the Divine Word (2) in your heart, being a victim in union with Him. You must be like Little Thérèse (3) an apostle of sorrowful love, a host-soul, immolated on behalf of the Church, forgetful of yourself. What a beautiful mission for which no one will ever be grateful enough! But remember, no one can be an apostle or have the role of a priest without being a MARTYR. LIVE ON THE CROSS! Such is the vocation of love's victims, the apostleship of the CROSS or on the CROSS is always infallible, it is the most fruitful and powerful, because it is that of true love. And this should be that of the "Oasis."

It is necessary, my dear daughter Teresa, that you fill your heart with Jesus, getting rid of everything that is earthly, for the earth is everything that Jesus is not. Realize that Jesus, and ONLY JESUS, is the Love which lasts. Let your heart be a ciborium, a lunette, a chalice FILLED WITH JESUS, a shell which overflows, all love, all suffering, so that this liqueur falls upon souls. You must earn for them the dew of grace, even though you do not see it, even if you do not know it. May God be glorified through your sacrifice, and that is enough.

This is true love, to be ANOTHER JESUS, but Jesus like HE IS, covered with blood, tears, humiliations, sorrows. "The lance, an author says, did not open the wound in Jesus' Heart, it only set aside the veil that covered it, because He was born with His Heart already WOUNDED BY LOVE." What a precious thought which is a reality! Saint Francis de Sales says that if they had performed an autopsy on Our Lord, it would have found that His death resulted from His Heart, that is, HIS LOVE. This is Jesus who used and, in that sense, ABUSED His omnipotence to suffer. Then, what are we doing, what are we thinking so much about, that this love does not move us? Unfortunately, we do not understand Jesus' infinite, eternal love, which does not tire, does not change, does not weaken, NOR DIE!

Well then make the resolution today to be NOTHING for CREATURES, NOTHING for yourself, and ALL FOR GOD. The great secret of holiness, I repeat to you, is TO LOVE, and saints are nothing but chalices of sorrowful love, "fools of faith, beings of light." Another day I will speak to you about the MARTYRDOM OF LOVE, that which most crucifies, and obtains the most graces. For now you have enough to entertain yourself at the feet of Jesus. I only tell you that humble souls are the ones who know how to love truly, and are the only ones to receive and communicate the rays of sovereign goodness.

Love, then, but with a love born of humility; we are not holy because WE ARE NOT HUMBLE. Do you love Me more than these? Tell Him: "This is what I desire, Jesus of my heart, this is what I long for with all the enthusiasm of my humble heart. To love You more than all the angels and saints." To love You, to love You! All the rest is detail, Jesus, images that pass, they are smoke that vanishes, only You, Jesus, Jesus and Mary. I want to enter into Your Heart, more deeply than the lance, more profoundly than Your Heartbeats, and live from its warmth and its light, its charity and zeal, its meekness and humility. That wound bleeds, that wound is waiting for me and hopes that I may be the balm that heals the ingratitude of the world and of those who are His own. You, the Jesus Who lives and breathes not far away, but right near to me, the One Whom I devour with the inmost ardent desire every morning, shall be, from now on, the confidant of my secrets, of my confidences.

You love me, and this electrifies me. You want to be my Father, my Guide, my Companion, my Brother, my Friend, my Spouse, my Everything! O sweet Jesus, LOOK AT ME! One glance from You, and my heart will be opened to holy growth. Give me Your Heartbeats, give me Your Voice, Your Heart, Your Tenderness, Your Compassion!

Possess me, absorb me, transform me, divinize me, simplifying me so that we may be two in one, You in me, I in You! Assume your little way, Teresa, make yourself small and LOVE, LOVE, and do not ask to be loved but ONLY TO LOVE.

Pray for me!

(L.R., Vol. IV/76-80)

(1) Mrs. Armida did not study theology, but she received from the Lord a special sensitivity to grasp spiritual matters. She recorded admirably what she heard in sermons and retreats.

(2) The "offering of the Divine Word to the Heavenly Father" is the central accomplishment of the Chain of Love (Golden Chain), a practice of the spiritual priesthood, peculiar to the Works of the Cross.

(3) Saint Thérèse of Lisieux, not yet canonized at the time.

36

August 9, 1924

My dearest daughter, Teresa de María:

How lovely is your Mistress, Mary! Listen! yesterday Mater (1) sent me your note and a letter from Mother Dolores (2) that must have crossed mine. What is happening to you? The cross of infirmities has visited you: stomach, malaria, hemorrhage, weakness. But this? Blessed be the Lord! Where does this fear of what they might bring you come from? What a "Madame Fortuneteller": before things ever happen, she foresees them, and afflicts herself, and mulls them over, and cries, red eyes, anguish, etc., all over something that might be, not knowing if it ever will be. First of all, Consuelo (3) has not written anything to me yet, and even if she wrote to me that the climate might suit you: are you mine, or do you belong to me? What foolishness, my God! Mother Ana (4) will do whatever she decides is suitable before God and that is all. I have never felt her eager to bring you here: I do not believe they will bring Mother Dolores either; all of this suffering for nothing.

Today I went to Mirto (5) for a half day retreat and saw Mother and she told me about your problems and that she has no plans to bring you here, unless you should become very ill and it was necessary, but I hope not. Perhaps the Lord gave you this little jolt, so that you can love Mother Dolores more, since I have no way to repay her kindness to you. I wrote Primitivo to send her $30.00 for your medicines, I do not know if my letter was able to reach him there, I am going to see how I can send them to you, or write to Daniel to give them to you. Did you receive the typewriter ribbon? Let me know. Also tell me up to what month the $10.00 have been paid (6). Take it easy, with a smile on your face although you are in bed, and do not stray from the path of obedience. If the Lord wills to take you (even though you are still green), well, this would be your time, and be peaceful.

Do not add to Mater's grief. Write often to Mother Ana, you know how good she is to us: you cannot imagine how kind and thoughtful she is with me. Lupe greatly appreciated your letter. She is sending you a holy card of Thérèse tossing flowers. I am very busy finishing the *Dew for Purgatory* (7), and your mother who loves you, blesses you, and would like to come in October (8). I hope Mother Anita can also come.

Concepción
(L.R., Vol. III/129)

(1) Mother Javiera Perochena, Superior General since the Chapter of 1921.
(2) Mother Dolores Barroso Mato, Superior of the House of Monterrey, where Sister Teresa de María got sick.
(3) Mrs. Consuelo Sada de Garza, a friend of Mrs. Armida, who lived in Monterrey.
(4) Mother Ana de María Cabrera (see letter 32 note 2).
(5) 11 Mirto Street. House of the Sisters of the Cross, Mother House of the Congregation, built in the form of a Cross with the Chapel of the Heart in the center, as in the Cross of the Apostleship. This House was taken over temporarily in 1914 by the Government. In 1926, it was definitely seized by the Government and turned into a School of Agriculture.
(6) Maybe a donation she sent to the House or a contribution for the candles for the adoration of the Blessed Sacrament, supported by benefactors, for whom the Sisters prayed during their terms of adoration night and day.
(7) *Rocío del Purgatorio*, a prayer book with practices, prayers and devotions on behalf of the deceased, Way of the Cross, etc., written by Mrs. Armida.
(8) To visit her in Monterrey, where her daughter was ill. Sister Teresa de María returned to Mexico City and continued being sick: she had Malta fever, sciatic pains and meningitis. By a special indult of the Archbishop of Mexico, she was assisted by her mother when she died in the House on Mirto Street on December 19, 1925. She suffered much. We can appreciate in this letter the prudence and tact of Mrs. Armida, in the way she shows understanding and love for her religious daughter on the one hand, and on the other, how she exhorts and encourages her to offer up her ailments and also reminds her of her place with respect to her religious superiors.

To Her Son Ignacio Armida y Cabrera

Ignacio Armida Cabrera, fifth son of Concepción Cabrera de Armida and Francisco Armida García, was born at 1 Juárez Street, in San Luis Potosí on Saturday, April 8, 1893, at five in the afternoon in the house of his maternal grandmother.

On July 8, 1919, in Mexico City — where the family had lived since 1895 — he married Isabel Morán y Bolaños Cacho from Oaxaca. Born on May 11, 1896, she died on August 30, 1940, leaving her husband with eight children, all of them born in Mexico City (José Ignacio had died on the day of his birth; Ignacio had died when he was six months old), Manuel, Ignacio, Carlos, Concepción, Jacobo, Isabel, Guillermo, and Consuelo, the youngest one, who entered the Order of the Sacred Heart on June 7, 1956. All married and Don Ignacio enjoyed having his huge family of children, in-laws, and grandchildren all around him on Sundays — in the same house where his mother lived with them during the last years of her life, and where she died on March 3, 1937: 16 Altavista, San Angel, Mexico City.

Ignacio died on June 30, 1979.

He was very kind to his mother. He accompanied her on her trip to the Holy Land and Rome in 1913, along with his youngest sister, Guadalupe. Concepción loved her daughter-in-law Chabela as a true daughter. As stated previously, she lived with them during the last years of her life. Her daughter-in-law cared for her and attended to her with filial tenderness; she died shortly after her mother-in-law.

After all his children were married and the youngest daughter entered the convent, Ignacio continued to live in the same house. Mrs. Armida had occupied a bedroom and a sitting room on the first floor, and in the cellar she had her praying room. She had asked Ignacio to come and give her a kiss whenever he would arrive, no matter what time it was. One night he stayed up late playing a little poker. He entered quietly and did not find her in her bedroom, and he went silently down to the cellar where he saw her carrying a cross and crowned with thorns. When she became weaker, she was moved to another bedroom on the second floor, where she died. Ignacio arranged a praying room there in memory of his mother. He warmly received visitors and with great affection he recalled memories of his mother: her luncheons, her trip to the Holy Land, his adventures as a young man in Paris and the vigilance of his mother, the visits she received from priests and bishops; taking her to the train and picking her up when she went to Morelia for her spiritual exercises, the sale of her books. In the end, during the last years of her life, this was the son who lived in greatest intimacy with her.

37

August 12, 1911

My dear Nachito, son of my soul:

If I should die, if I should die (1) if Our Lord wills to take me, I beg you not to forget my advice. Before everything else, be a good Christian; go to Communion often, have a great, great love for the Blessed Virgin, have a Mass said in her honor every month, and commend your enterprises and your future to her. Do not go young and alone to the United States or to Europe.

If the Lord destines you to married life, consult Him, and approach the altar keeping your chastity. Be very pure in thoughts, words and deeds. Be an example for your younger brothers and sister, give them good advice, be patient with them, do not have noticeable preferences between Pablo (2) and Salvador (3). I especially ask you to take good care of Lupe (4). For Corona (5) charity, and affection. Be the leader of the house if you stay and live with your brothers, and pay attention to the servants, that they all accomplish their religious duties. Go to confession frequently and never go to sleep in a state of sin.

Be good in whatever status of life God establishes you. Believe me, I have always loved you very much and if I have been strict in some points, it has been for your own good. Good-bye, son of my soul, until heaven, I will await you there, make yourself worthy to go there loving the Lord with all your heart, being an exemplary Christian and living in great unity with Pancho (6) and your brothers and sister.

Do not become too desirous of acquiring riches and do not think only about money; remember your soul. All earthly things are worth little and we might have to leave them soon; rather, heap up treasures for heaven; have a spiritual director to whom you may confide all your sorrows and do not forget me in your prayers. I await you over there, I will come for you, but behave as my beloved son whom I love so. You mother blesses you with all her soul.

Concepción
(L.R., Vol. I/50-51)

(1) At this time, Mrs. Armida was ill and several times she thought she was dying (*Spiritual Diary* 35/466). On this occasion she wrote her son Ignacio who was then the elder brother at home, as Francisco had married the preceding year.

(2) Pablo Armida y Cabrera. He developed typhus and died on June 27, 1913, at the age of eighteen.

(3) Salvador Armida y Cabrera married Amada Gutiérrez del Torno. They did not have any children. He died in Coyoacán, Ave María 8, Mexico City, on December 2, 1975.

(4) Guadalupe Armida y Cabrera, who married Carlos Lafarga y Aragón on May 15, 1924.

(5) Coronación Cabrera Sotomayor, daughter of her brother Juan Cabrera y Arias. She lived for a time in the house of Mrs. Armida.

(6) Francisco Armida y Cabrera, the eldest brother, married to Elisa Baz y Duclaud in 1910.

38

June 15, 1919

Nachito, my dear son:

I have not forgotten you. Can one forget the person she loves? I have prayed a lot for you. And do you know what I am asking for you? Humility, a meekness of judgment for the sake of your own happiness. Sometimes you are by character stubborn in your judgments and opinions; remember, my son, only fools never change and you are not one of them. Remove that small defect which is a tiny blemish on your soul which has so many other virtues and qualities. You are also proud; what happened with M.L. proved it to me. Who pays attention to clouds that go by? Detest such childish behavior and forget those silly things of which life is filled.

You must acquire the virtues you are lacking and develop the ones you have to make Chabela happy (1) so as to create a blest and holy home for her. Reflect, "Without leaving aside what we are, we are able to be what we are not with the Lord's help." I want to help you in your marriage because I believe Chabela is going to make you happy, as far as one can be on earth. I so want you to take to the altar, if not a material fortune, virtues which she will appreciate for she is also virtuous.

So now, amend your ways. Understand? Be more pious, because only God can overcome your difficulties and help you to reach your goal. He loves you very much, you are His pet and you, having Him in your own house (2), hardly pay any attention to Him. Is this not ingratitude? Why not get up and serve Mass, at least every other day? By sacrificing a few minutes of laziness as you do when going to a game, etc. What a shame and how little thoughtfulness towards Him Who gave you Chabela as a fiancée and Who will give her to you as a spouse if you are faithful. Why not pray the Rosary daily?

Your life now must revolve around God and your fiancée, being faithful to her. AND WHAT ABOUT YOUR MOTHER? She will be satisfied staying on the sidelines as long as you are happy. So now, then, cling fast to the Blessed Virgin, LOVE HER A LOT for she is your mother and she will bless your marriage with her purity and her affection. Goodbye, my son. What joyous days I have spent in solitude (3) praying for Chabela and you and for my poor soul. I really needed it. Also, another recommendation I give to you is that you LEARN ABOUT YOUR RELIGION. It is so beautiful! Every day a little, and you will make much progress. Your mother embraces you and blesses you with all her soul.

Concepción
(L.R., Vol. I/52-55)

(1) Isabel Morán Bolaños Cacho, from Oaxaca. The marriage took place on July 8, 1919, in Mexico City.
(2) Archbishop Ramón Ibarra y González had obtained from Pope Pius X in 1913 the privilege of having the Blessed Sacrament in her oratory.
(3) Mrs. Armida made the spiritual exercises of Saint Ignatius from May 10 to June 8, 1919. For her meditations, she followed some notes that her Jesuit brother, Primitivo, let her have. He also visited her sometimes to complete the meditations.

39

Coyoacán, Thursday, January 27, 1921

My dear Nachín:

At last we received your letter which we had been anxiously expecting. It is almost eight days since you left. Thank God that nothing serious happened to Belita (1); take good care of her. I am glad you arrived on time to see Sebastian's corpse (2). What a strange disease! He died because God wanted him to die, that is all!

We were so pleased to realize how much they loved him; he really deserved it and he sowed to reap. God knows how to give a reward even in our earthly life. The solemn funeral rites are very beautiful: it is a music that soaks through to the bones and conducts the soul to serious thoughts of the afterlife. How many suffrages he must have had, on top of the material and moral purification of his illness. How much he must have suffered and without being able to speak!

May God keep him in His kingdom. I am going to send your letter to Carmela (3) so she may learn the details. What you say about Conchita (4) does not surprise me. I appreciate her for her worth; she is a soul the Lord loves for Himself! Everyone sends regards, and I send you a big hug.

Concepción

When are you coming? There is no sympathy stationery (5) here. Tell me when you're coming so I can make plans.

(L.R., Vol. I/56-57)

(1) Isabel Morán y Bolaños Cacho, the wife of Ignacio Armida Cabrera.

(2) Sebastián Blanco, husband of Concepción Morán y Bolaños Cacho, sister of Isabel. They had three boys: one of them, Guillermo, married and two became Jesuit priests, Jacobo and Luciano, missionaries in the Tarahumara.

(3) Carmen Morán y Bolaños Cacho, sister of Concepción and Isabel. She entered the Congregation of the Sisters of the Cross of the Sacred Heart of Jesus and took the name of María Teresa del Niño Jesús. She was Directress of Novices and Superior General. They also had a Jesuit brother, Fr. Jacobo Morán y Bolaños Cacho.

(4) Concepción Morán y Bolaños Cacho, the widow of Sebastián Blanco. Father Primitivo Cabrera met the Morán family in Oaxaca when he was a missionary there, and it was he who introduced them to Mrs. Armida.

(5) It was the custom in those days to use paper bordered in black when someone in the family had died or when writing a note of sympathy to a family in mourning.

40

July 30, 1934

My dear son Ignacio:

I send you my congratulations for tomorrow with heart and soul and desire your happiness, asking for you, more so even than usual, that He may fill you with His special blessing and His divine love. You cannot imagine how sorry I am not to be with you on your saint's day and not to play the "mañanitas" for you (1); you cannot imagine how hard it was for me to have to return here before your saint's day and your dental appointment. God knows how hard it was for me to leave, but circumstances required it (even though I kept delaying my coming here); may the Lord accept my sacrifice for your sake.

I hope you have a very happy saint's day, son of my soul, surrounded by your Chabelita and your children; I will spend the day at the foot of the Tabernacle asking for many things for you and for your dear ones, who are also mine. I will give you your gift when I return; the spiritual one will be the biggest I can manage in favor of your dear soul.

I suppose that on Wednesday they will pull your teeth, as you thought, I SHALL NOT FORGET YOU: go to confession even if there is no danger, and I beg you to let me know immediately, that same day, even if only through a post card, how you came out of it and how you are.

I sent you a post card on Saturday. I am better, without fatigue even when I walk; maybe it is because of the lower altitude here (2). The doctor (3) comes everyday; you know how considerate the Bishop (4) and also Angela (5) are. I am worried about Pancho (6) and will keep calm until he gets back.

So, Nachín, a thousand blessings from your mother, who envelops you with her memories, love and prayers. A thousand things to Chabela and kisses for your five and regards to Nena (7). A thousand hugs, goodbye.

Concepción

P.S. And what about the mangoes you offered me?

(L.R., Vol. I/64-65)

(1) A popular song to congratulate dear persons or relatives on their saint's day. It is generally sung early in the morning to wake that person with music.

(2) Mrs. Armida was in Morelia making her yearly retreat. This year she began it on July 28 and finished it on August 28. Coming back to Mexico City, she went through León, visited the Sisters of the Cross there, and also went by Celaya. These were the eighth spiritual exercises that Bishop Martínez guided for her. The theme was "To offer Jesus up to be crucified."

(3) Doctor Florentino Villalón, from Morelia.

(4) Luis María Martínez, Bishop of Morelia and afterwards Primate Archbishop of Mexico. He was her spiritual director from July 7, 1925, to March 3, 1937, the day that she died in a saintly manner. He used to take her to his house for the meditations.

(5) Miss Angela Rodríguez, aunt of Bishop Martínez, who took care of his house following the death of Mrs. Ramona Rodríguez.

(6) Her son Francisco Armida y Cabrera, who might have been on a business trip, as it was necessary for his establishment.

(7) Maybe little Isabel.

41

August 1, 1934

SPECIAL DELIVERY
Mr. Ignacio Armida
29 Juárez Avenue
Coyoacán, Mexico City

My dear son Nacho:

From the very beginning of the day thinking about you and imagining the dentist's office, the chair, the gas, your fright, your nerves, poor thing! Etc. etc. I am tempted to send you a telegram, but I thought that possibly the removal of your teeth was not today.

I did not forget you all day long yesterday. How did you spend it? Did you receive my letter? In my place, pretend that I am the book, *Jesus, What Is He Really Like?* (1), and I ask you to read one or two of its chapters each day. The first two are the heaviest ones, the others are not. So imagine me at your side.

These people here are so good to me. I have been better with the climate and the quiet and my nearness to Him. I am sending you a prayer of the Virgin of the Lightning. Pray it with great fervor; I shall look for its history.

A thousand regards, and your mother who is not far away from you, embraces you.

Concepción
(L.R., Vol. I/66)

(1) In this book, she speaks chapter by chapter of the different aspects and virtues of Jesus. Her great desire was to make Him known so that He might be loved the more. The first two chapters are "His Divinity" and "His Love for the Father."

42

September 17, 1934

Mr. Ignacio Armida
P.O. Box 2650
Mexico City

My dear son Nacho:

Today is the 33rd anniversary of the death of your father, God rest his soul. I hope you have remembered him and have prayed for his soul.

I am suffering from terrible neuralgias; they become worse at night and keep me sitting up until three in the morning. I can hardly wait for them to extract all the teeth I have left.

On the 19th, at night, this is the day after tomorrow, I am leaving with Father Edmundo (1) so I will arrive on Thursday morning. I am so sorry that you have to get up so early, but what else can we do? How are the Chabelitas (2) getting along? I am dying to see the baby! I am so happy for Conchita! (3) I am expecting your news today. I also learned that Pepe Armida (4) also received a Teresita these days.

So a big hug for Chabela, another for you and regards and kisses for the children. Until a little later, your mother who embraces you.

Concepción

I received the medicines. Thank you. Please add to the account of the other invoices.

(L.R., Vol. I/67)

(1) Father Edmundo Iturbide, M.Sp.S., from Morelia. Vicar of Fr. Félix Rougier and Superior General of the Congregation after him.

(2) Isabel Morán y Bolaños Cacho and her newly born daughter Isabel Armida Morán.

(3) Concepción Armida y Morán, the only little girl among five boys.

(4) José Armida y Torres, son of Ildefonso Armida y García, a brother of Concepción's husband and Damiana Torres, from Jalapa. He was married to Concepción Velasco Taboada. This is their second daughter. See letters 87, 88, 89, 90.

43

To Her Daughter-in-Law
Isabel Morán Bolaños Cacho
Wife of Her Son Ignacio

Mexico, February 17, 1917

My dear Chabela:

You realize what a deep sorrow the Lord has sent to us, especially to me, because Bishop Ibarra was truly a father to me; he was also my spiritual director and the founder and protector of the Works of the Cross (1). He came to spend a few days here and the Lord wanted me to witness the death of a saint, that we might receive from him heroic examples of virtue. Blessed be God for everything!

This is the reason I had not written to thank you for the lovely things you sent to me for Our Lord (2). The covers for the ciborium, so well made and of such good taste! Wonderful hands of my Chabelita! May God keep them and may He reward you for this precious gift. Everyone liked them. Also Lupe's present, the sewing kit, is darling. Why did you go to all this trouble?

Just imagine! Today they sent Concha to the House of Puebla (3); God's will. Carmela (4) is going to miss her very much. I had the pleasure of meeting Tomás (5); he came to pay us a visit and I asked him to give you my regards. By mail I am sending you the little book (6) for Communion, that famous one Carmela typed.

Your soul friend embraces you tenderly, with regards to everybody.

Concepción

Lupe is better, keep praying that she be cured.

(L.R., Vol. I/76-77)

(1) Ramón Ibarra y González, first Archbishop of Puebla. Spiritual director of Mrs. Armida from October 1912, to February 1, 1917, the day of his death. He was also Father of the Works of the Cross; he promoted the Apostleship of the Cross and erected Crosses of the Apostleship in his diocese. He obtained the permits and indulgences for the Apostleship, the Covenant of Love with the Sacred Heart of Jesus, the approvals of the Religious of the Cross, the foundation of the Missionaries of the Holy Spirit, and of the Priestly Fraternity. His cause of Canonization has already been introduced in Rome. Statements that Mrs. Armida gives about him in this letter are important.

(2) Mrs. Armida had the Blessed Sacrament in her home. Bishop Ibarra also obtained this permit for her from Pope St. Pius X. She took exquisite care of the Blessed Sacrament and that is why she is so grateful to Chabela for her present.

(3) Concepción Armida y Cabrera, Sister of the Cross, who took the name of Teresa de María Inmaculada. She was sent by her superiors to the House of Puebla founded by Bishop Ramón Ibarra González, a double separation for Mrs. Armida. The Lord told her that she had begun a period of solitude, and she must accompany and imitate Mary Most Holy during the years she survived her divine Son on the earth. This is a special devotion to Our Lady, and in a certain way a new one, which the Works of the Cross must live and spread.

(4) Carmen Morán y Bolaños Cacho, sister of Isabel. A Sister of the Cross who took the name of María Teresa del Niño Jesús. As a young lady she was sent to Mrs. Armida by her brother Primitivo, Jesuit missionary, for he saw signs of a religious vocation in her. She lived in Mrs. Armida's home. A deep and tender affection for each other grew in them. She became Superior, Directress of Novices, member of the General Council of the Congregation, and finally Superior General for two successive periods, from 1955 to 1967. She died as a General Counselor in the General House of Coyoacán, Mexico City on October 10, 1969. She wrote some religious poems and also a biographical sketch of Mrs. Armida.

(5) Tomás Morán y Bolaños Cacho, brother of Chabela and Carmen.

(6) Probably the book *Chispitas de Amor* (*Sparks of Love*), prayers of thanksgiving following Communion.

44

July 8, 1933

Dear Chabelita:

My congratulations on this day that I had hoped to spend with you, but Escobar (1) will not let me walk. Besides, the day before yesterday when I was taking my bath, I slipped on the cement when I was going to close a window and I fell on one foot. I have a black-and-blue toe and Escobar said it had been spillage from a vein: the issue is that it really hurts me a lot, my foot has swollen and I cannot put on my shoe.

How are you feeling? Is it true that Chita (2) is coming? Teresa (3) is dying to see her. I am sending you a gelatin, $10.00, and some bottles of wine from Mrs. Aymes (4) and above all, a big embrace with my love and gratitude. Primitivo tells me he is coming for the 12th. I hope to be there by then.

Take good care of yourself, and even though you think you are feeling better, please do not work too much! You might be injured for the rest of your life. Many kisses to your five and I embrace you.

Concepción

Manuela (5) C. García (6), Guadalupe (7), Lola Alcorta (8), and Catita (9), send their congratulations. By the way, Chabelita, empty the gelatin on a round platter, as it is on ice and you must loosen it with your fingers and shake it. The cream goes in the center. I will leave Wednesday morning or Tuesday night (10). DO NOT COME DOWN.

(L.R., Vol. I/72)

(1) Doctor Leopoldo Escobar, married to Carmen Lafarga, sister of Carlos, husband of Lupe Armida y Cabrera.

(2) Concepción Morán y Bolaños Cacho, a widow of Sebastián Blanco (see letter 39).

(3) Carmen Morán y Bolaños Cacho, in religious life María Teresa del Niño Jesús, R.C.S.C.J.

(4) Mrs. Valentina Aymes, a very spiritual and apostolic lady, she founded the "Cadettes du Christ" for pious young ladies. She was a friend of Mrs. Armida, and gave her presents. She died in the Saint Vincent Residence of the Sisters of Charity. She had lost a leg. She suffered as a very good Christian woman. Correspondence between them is preserved.

(5) R.M. Manuela Cacho Ordozgoiti, R.C.S.C.J., Superior General.

(6) Mother Concepción García, R.C.S.C.J.

(7) Mother Guadalupe Monterrubio, R.C.S.C.J.

(8) Mother Dolores Alcorta, R.C.S.C.J., sister of Luis Alcorta, member of the "Liga de los Cristeros."

(9) Mother Catalina García, R.C.S.C.J.

(10) Mrs. Armida wrote this letter from the House of the Sisters of the Cross of the Sacred Heart of Jesus. She had had heart trouble. She also helped her daughter Guadalupe to take care of her son Carlos, who had been operated on and had erysipelas.

45

November 16, 1933

Dear Chabelita:

Guess what! That the chapter "His Soul" in the book (1) *Jesus, What Is He Really Like?* is missing! I beg you to look in the drawers of the desk for the sheets, in the bundle of rough drafts. It is in a drawer: it is already typed. If you do not find it, ask in Tacubaya (2) if, by chance, they did not leave it there. It is one of those that I put together at the last moment. They are going to print the book, Father Treviño (3) tells me.

Did they remove the Blessed Sacrament? (4) Octa (5) is very weak; the doctor is frightened; right now he feels cold; let us see if we can keep him warm; he cannot move, sleep, or eat. Is Primitivo there? My regards to Nacho, for him a thousand things, and kisses for your five; every one here sends you all regards. Tere (6) is well and happy.

Concepción
(L.R., Vol. I/82)

(1) One of the chapters of the book she had written.

(2) The house of the Sisters of the Cross on Tránsito Street in Tacubaya. They had typed this work.

(3) Father Guadalupe Treviño, who ran the publishing house, "La Cruz," for more than fifty years. Born in Santa Clara, Michoacán, he died on Thursday, April 21, 1983, after a very fruitful life as a priest, spiritual director, writer, and editor.

(4) She had, as we have already said, permission to keep the Blessed Sacrament in her home.

(5) Octaviano Cabrera y Arias, her brother, who was ill in San Luis Potosí. She went there to see and be with him. He was ill for fifty days and died on December 27, 1933.

(6) Little Teresa Lafarga Armida, her granddaughter; a daughter of Guadalupe Armida and Carlos Lafarga. She had accompanied her to San Luis.

46

November 20, 1933

Father Félix's Saint's Day
Mrs. Isabel M. de Armida
29 Juárez Ave.
Coyoacán, Mexico City

My dear Chabelita:

I received your letter and I hope Prisci (1) came, so you do not have to do all the work: could you hire Petra or Enriqueta (2) in the meanwhile? Let me know about the expenses. In the chest of drawers in front of the W.C. there should be linen for the beds, the sheets I marked for Primitivo.

I found "His Soul," — not the revised one — and I sent it certified to Father Guadalupe (3) to 24 Juárez Avenue. I beg you to see if it arrived; you know how difficult the certified mail is and I am pressed to know; and please answer me in a post card. Sofía (4) tells me that they went for the books.

A thousand things to Nacho and kisses for your five. I embrace you.

Concepción

Octa continues to be ill.

(L.R., Vol. I/83)

(1) Prisciliana, a servant of Mrs. Armida.
(2) Two servants of the family.
(3) Father Guadalupe Treviño (see letter 45).
(4) Mother Sofía Garduño, foundress of the Catechists of the Sacred Hearts of Jesus and Mary: "Violetas." Sponsored by Bishop Guillermo Tritchler y Córdoba. This Institute began on May 12, 1918. Mother Sofía died on Palm Sunday 1977. Mrs. Armida appreciated her very much. This religious took care of her during her last illness and wrapped her in her shroud. She testified during the exhumation of the mortal remains of Mrs. Armida.

47

Mrs. Isabel M. de Armida
29 Juárez Ave.
Coyoacán, Mexico City

My dear Chabelita:

Thank you for so kindly taking care of all my bothersome requests. I am waiting for the book for Holy Week (1) and *Before the Altar* in French (2). Did you send the books to Mexicali? They are urgently asking for them.

By the way, please send me a box of face powder, the one Tula (3) bought for me. "Mil Flores" ("A Thousand Flowers") burns my face.

I'd also like the book of the *Repentant Woman* by return mail. It is black and is in the small bookcase in the entry. A thousand regards to Nacho. Kisses to your five and I embrace you.

Concepción

Did you write Prisci (4) not to come?

(L.R., Vol. I/85)

---

(1) A book of devotions for Holy Week.
(2) Her book *Before the Altar, Visits to the Blessed Sacrament*, is the first one she wrote. She signed the books that followed: "By the author of *Before the Altar.*" It was translated into several languages, first into French by Father Félix Rougier.
(3) Gertrudis Parcero, a young lady who studied with the Dominican Sisters for ten years. She lived with Mrs. Armida for a time. She entered the Institute of the Catechists of the Sacred Hearts of Jesus and Mary "Violetas," founded by Mother Sofia Garduño (see letter 46). Gertrudis entered the convent in 1929 and died in 1933.
(4) Prisciliana, servant of Mrs. Armida.

48

Mrs. Isabel M. de Armida
29 Juárez Ave.
Coyoacán, Mexico City

My dear children Nacho and Chabela:

I am in the midst of mourning and will finish on the 24th, so I will leave on the 27th. I will advise you RIGHT ON TIME, as Nacho says.

How are you feeling, Chabelita? I was very sorry to learn of your illness.

Tomorrow the Delegate (1) will arrive. Tell me how you are getting along, and also Carlitos (2). By the way, give $5 to Refugio (3) for whatever she needs.

Here I am sending you the recipe for the buñuelos; pass it on to Lupe. To half a kilo of flour you add two yolks and a whole egg and three tablespoons of lard. You moisten the pastry with tepid water, boiled with the peel of green tomatoes, (4) anise, a little piece of rock salt (5) and sweeten it. Knead it until it makes "eyes," let it rest in the form of a ball, or out in the sun for a while smeared with lard, then spread it out with a wooden roll and with a glass cup you fashion the dough and extend it and fry them in $1 worth of lard. The gaznates (6) come out well with this dough, only cut them out with a small pastry wheel (7), and press the ends together with a little bit of egg white. I hope you enjoy them.

Say, please make the dessert of purple sweet potato for me. My rheumatism is doing better now. Until later. Tell Nacho I have prayed to the Lord for him.

Conce
(L.R., Vol. I/86)

(1) The Archbishop of Morelia and Apostolic Delegate in Mexico, Leopoldo Ruíz y Flores, a great protector of the Works of the Cross and adviser of Mrs. Armida. He is the person by whom the most letters were preserved.

(2) Carlos Armida y Morán, son of Nacho and Chabela. The third of the living children.

(3) A servant.

(4) A small green tomato that is wrapped in a covering which is boiled for preparing these buñuelos, a fried pastry special for Christmas time.

(5) A limestone used in boiling the corn for the nixtamal. It has the same effect as baking soda.

(6) Another fried pastry like a hollow roll, made with the same dough and filled with cream or meringue.

(7) A little wheel that cuts dough for cookies. Triangles, squares or strips can be cut. For these "gaznates" strips are then cut crosswise, joined at the ends, fried, and then stuffed with cream or meringue or sprinkled with sugar.

To Her Son Salvador Armida y Cabrera

Salvador Armida y Cabrera, the seventh son of Concepción Cabrera and Francisco Armida, was born in Mexico City on Friday, June 19, 1896 at noon, on El Tompeate Street, which is an extension of Alfaro Street.

He married Amada Gutiérrez y del Torno, daughter of Juan Gutiérrez and María del Torno, on September 24, 1929. They did not have children. Before marrying Salvador lived with his mother. When her last son married, Mrs. Armida went to live with her son Ignacio and her daughter-in-law Chabela and their children. They first lived at 29 Juárez Ave. in Coyoacán; afterwards they moved to San Angel, 16 Altavista Street, where Mrs. Armida died a holy death.

Salvador worked with his brother Francisco in the Casa Armida, a store for typewriters and other office furniture, founded by his elder brother. They struggled bravely to keep it going, even during the economic crisis of the 30's.

He died on December 2, 1975 in his home at 8 Ave María St., in Coyoacán, Mexico City.

49

June 16, 1931

My dear son Salva:

I came away very unhappy because of the quarrel on Sunday. Oh, my Good God! It is very sad that this occurs in a family and I beg you to heal this wound, that you cure this scar, but from the depth of your heart. There were fits of temper (1) on both your parts and you must bury these things, they are like clouds which pass. I do not want love and confidence to become clouded in the family, and much less between brothers and sisters. You know how Lupe is, she is very passionate and does not even think what she says: but down in the bottom of her heart, she is good and sincere. So forgive each other because this is what ought to be, and to make me happy. Do NOT BECOME ESTRANGED FROM EACH OTHER, because then unity will become more difficult. Invite her to eat or to something else, and promise me that everything will be as before (2). Chabela wrote to me that she had a bilious spell. Go to see her. I hope to go back on Saturday, or at the latest on Monday.

I have had bile trouble and terrible rheumatism in my back. Everyone sends their regards to you and Amadita (3). Your birthday will be on the 19th, and I will not forget you. You mother kisses you and blesses you.

Concep.

So the business is still going badly? God's will!

(L.R., Vol. II/77)

(1 "Prontos" in familiar language, fits of temper.
(2) Mrs. Armida's appeasing spirit is remarkable in this letter, as is her energetic personality. She wants to reconcile her children no matter what; they have noble but impetuous characters.
(3) Amada Gutiérrez y del Torno, wife of Salvador Armida y Cabrera.

50

1932

My dearest son Salva: (1)

I beg you to keep on being a very good husband, to practice your religion and my counsels until death. May human respect never mislead you from your faith, because only this can make you happy and make la Chatita (2) also happy.

When Nacho can pay what I lent him, I have already told him to give you a fourth part, and if the business survives and something is left for me, you will also have a fourth part. If I were to have more, I would gladly give it to you.

I will expect you in heaven; be patient and brave in your illnesses and work, everything passes away and a joyous eternity awaits us. Never cease receiving the Sacraments. Your mother blesses you.

Concepción
(L.R., Vol. II/64)

(1) During a serious illness in this year of 1932, Mrs. Armida wrote this testament to her son Salvador (Salva or Salvita), a letter in which she blends spiritual and practical advice with dispositions regarding her finances. Her insistence in asking her children to receive the Sacraments frequently and to behave as good Christians and not to be ashamed of practicing their religion is outstanding in this period during which Mexico was going through a religious persecution. She also insists on the accomplishment of the duties deriving from their state in life.

(2) This is what they called Amada Gutiérrez y del Torno, the wife of Salvador Armida y Cabrera. A familiar nickname, "short nose."

51

Without a date

My dear son Salva: (1)

Now that the Lord has made you happy with Amadita, be a model husband, instruct yourselves more and more in our religion, and if God does give you children, take good care of their souls (2).

I mean that if the business survives and the store is put back on the right track (3) of what I have there, divide it evenly between yourselves. Do not be wordly. Do not criticize, for the Lord is all Love. Think that you are going to die, and live as fervent Christians, always loving your religion.

Salvita, do not forget me in your prayers, and I entrust to you a GREAT UNION among your brothers and sister (4). Be a MESSENGER OF PEACE. Thank the Lord for the wife He has given you, and make her happy by forming a Holy Christian home.

Your mother who expects you in heaven, blesses you.

Concepción
(L.R., Vol. II/86)

---

(1) In this other letter-testament (see previous letter 50) without a date, she must have been seriously ill, and addresses these lines to him. Besides the themes that were noted regarding the previous letter, in this one she recommends religious instruction, another point on which she always insisted with her children.

(2) They did not have children. Mrs. Armida was sorry about this, and in a letter to her son, Manuel, the Jesuit priest, she asked him to pray for this intention. She was highly interested in the education of the children, especially in what concerned the spiritual.

(3) The "Casa Armida," a business for typewriters and office supplies, founded by Francisco Armida y Cabrera, the eldest son, and in which the other brothers — Ignacio, Salvador, and the husband of Guadalupe, Carlos

Lafarga — worked. In the 30's they suffered an economic crisis due to the dollar exchange and they were in fear of bankruptcy. They were able to withstand the situation and maintain the business.

(4) She also enjoins them not to be worldly and to practice charity and, over all, unity, something of capital importance to her which she recommended throughout her letters to her children. She must have given it great significance and she advises them upon this theme of fraternal charity.

52

December 27, 1933

My dear children Salva and Amadita:

Thanks a million for your telegram of condolence. It has truly been a great grief for me to lose the one who was more than a brother (1): father, companion, friend, and counselor and father to my children. This house is finished, as everything will be on the earth. Happy are we for having faith and do not weep as those who have no hope! We shall see them again! How have you been? Salvita, are you passing near here on your hunting trip?

I am seeing about the day to go to Monterrey for eight days; they do not want me to go until the nine days are over (2), but I want to leave on Saturday, God willing. Primitivo was not able to be here for the day of the funeral. I went to the cemetery; I wanted to accompany him to the end. He died like a saint, longing for heaven. Pancho had a stroke night before last in the oratory, he fell on his face, he became pale and they had to carry him to bed. No telling if it was a bilious spell or his heart. Blessed be God for everything! God is love, all love, and even in His apparent harshness cannot be but love. A thousand regards to your family, Amadita, and I embrace you all.

Concepción

By the way, I am surprised that Nacho has not written to me; is he ill? (3)

(L.R., Vol. II/74-75)

---

(1) Her brother, Octaviano Cabrera y Arias (see letter 16).
(2) The nine days that were set aside for mourning, and the prayers recited on that occasion.
(3) In this letter one can appreciate both her feminine sensibility and her great spirit of faith in conformity with God's will and the hope of future life.

55

To Her Daughter-in-Law Amadita Gutiérrez Wife of Her Son Salvador

Morelia, September 12, 1934
Mrs. Amadita G. de Armida
Mexico City

My dearest Amadita:

Tomorrow will be your saint's day and through these lines I am sending you my congratulations, from the depths of my heart. You know how much I love you and the good things I wish for you. I will offer my Communion and all that I am able to, asking the Lord to fill your soul with His blessings. When we see each other, which will be soon, I will give you your gift, okay?

Yesterday I came from León and had to stay in Celaya because I could not make my train connection, and today I came here for another layover so as not to ascend all at once the 400 meters to Mexico's higher altitude. In León I felt very bad, and my heart was beating irregularly. I hope to leave here the 16th or the 17th, which is the anniversary of Pancho's death, my husband for 33 years! And it seems like yesterday; I also loved him dearly, like you love Salva.

I am worried about Chabela (1), I ask you to see about her, and I hope to arrive on time. To Salva, a thousand things from me; to your dear parents (2), Beca and Julio (3), Juanito and Lucha (4), my regards. And you, my dear Chatita (5) receive my regards, my love, and my humble prayers.

Concepción
(L.R., Vol. II/70-71)

(1) Isabel Morán y Bolaños Cacho, wife of Ignacio Armida y Cabrera, who was expecting a baby. Isabel Armida y Morán was born on September 14, 1934. She married Federico Mantilla y Montiel on November 25, 1965. They had three children, born in Mexico City: Federico, Gerardo, and Isabel.

(2) Juan Gutiérrez and María del Torno.

(3) Rebeca (Beca) Gutiérrez del Torno, sister of Amadita and her husband, Julio Zetina.

(4) Juan Gutiérrez del Torno, brother of Amadita, and his wife Luz.

(5) A familiar nickname they gave to Amadita.

54

October 26

My dear Amadita:

How have you been? and your parents, and the rest of the family? Give my very affectionate regards to everyone.

They say the "little house" is very nice; let us see to whom you dedicate it, and have Primitivo bless it for you. I will go to Mexico City at the middle or end of November.

I am very rested, but feel quite ill and moth eaten.

I embrace you with all my love as your mother-in-law.

Concepción
(L.R., Vol. II/82)

55

June 19, 1931?

My dear daughter Amadita:

I was very sorry about what you said Lupe told you, please forgive her; it's her temper. She says things and afterward she is sorry. Be of one heart and please do not distance yourself from her. These are clouds that quickly pass away. I entrust this especially to you because of your good heart and your tact.

I sent you a postcard. Did it arrive? I have been feeling badly; my hometown does not agree with me (1). Please do not fail to see Chabela. I intend to leave on Saturday or Sunday.

To your parents, Beca and Julio, Juan and Lucha, my regards and I say good-bye with a hug. (2)

Concepción
(L.R., Vol. II/84)

(1) San Luis Potosí.
(2) In this letter one can notice Mrs. Armida's conciliatory character; she tries to preserve peace within the family at any cost, and she has recourse to persuasion and tenderness. She also points out personal qualities and she excuses them.

To Her Married Daughter
Guadalupe Armida y Cabrera De Lafarga

Guadalupe Armida y Cabrera was born in Mexico City on Friday, February 11, 1898 on Montealegre Street, at noon (cf. *Autobiography*, Important dates).

She accompanied her mother, together with her brother Ignacio, on the pilgrimage to the Holy Land and Rome, which was organized and directed by Bishop Ramón Ibarra y González — since declared a Venerable Servant of God — to pray at the Holy Sites and in Rome for Mexico in the throes of revolution and persecution, and to take Mrs. Armida before the Sovereign Pontiff so as to obtain recognition for the foundation of the Missionaries of the Holy Spirit and the consolidation of the Works of the Cross.

On May 15, 1924, she married Carlos Lafarga y Aragón in Mexico City in the Church of Our Lady of Guadalupe Queen of Peace, on Enrico Martínez Street.

Carlos was born in March, 1893. They had two children, Teresa and Carlos, born in Mexico City; both of them married. Teresa married Constantino Madero y González and had two children: Teresa and Constantino. Carlos Lafarga y Armida married María de la Luz González y Rojo Matute and had three children, Carlos, Francisco Javier, and María de la Luz.

For a period of time, Mrs. Armida lived in an apartment next to Guadalupe's and sometimes spent the day at her house and helped her when either she or the children were ill.

Teresita also used to spend some time with her grandmother

and would accompany her on her trips to San Luis Potosí or Monterrey on the occasion of a marriage or death.

Lupe died in Mexico City on July 18, 1980.

56

To Her Daughter Guadalupe
(Incomplete)

In most unfortunate marriages, it is the woman's fault. When a woman crosses the threshold of marriage, she must leave her self with her self-love, her sensitivity and her egotism; she must become a sacrifice. There "she" must disappear so that "he" may enter peacefully and in a holy manner. Victory over self, docility, affability, prudence, tact, and foresight are the arms that a woman must display when she marries. In a home, in the state of matrimony, foresight is an indispensable virtue or quality that circumvents a great number of quarrels. The clouds in marriage may be dissipated through tact, prudence, and love, in the precious death of one's self. Flippancy is a very bad companion in matrimony, it must never raise its head in a Christian home, it can be the cause of many evils.

If a married woman must leave herself behind when she crosses the threshold of marriage, she must, on the other hand, bring to it a variety of moral virtues which must accompany her always and will help her on more than one occasion.

A married woman must not let her qualities be known, much less when they could overshadow her husband. She must never usurp his rights before society or herself, and even less before him.

A married woman must always ennoble the support that God gave her, even at the risk of being considered a fool. If her husband is not very bright, she must cover it up by buttressing this defect with her own talents and always building him up. We all have talents and defects. Matrimony is such a heavy cross that it can only be carried between the two, the day one of them lets go of it, the other one needs a powerful divine help to support it, and it must not be looked for in any other place (1).

(L.R., Vol. I/39–41)

(1) In this counsel which Mrs. Armida gives her daughter about marriage, one can feel, naturally, the influence of the customs of those times, but she presents valuable principles for all time. It is especially interesting because it reflects her own principles in her marriage, and these are backed up by the success of her marriage and of her family life. Mrs. Armida was profoundly feminine and she knew how to assume her responsibilities as a friend, as a wife, as a companion, and counselor of her husband, as a tender but also strict mother with her children, as a housekeeper; with her family, and in her societal life.

57

September 1932

My dear daughter Lupe (1):

Father Thomas (2) will give you 100 pesos each month as long as the money I left him for you lasts. When Ignacio is able to pay, I will give you one of the four parts he will make. If matters go better in the business, they will also give you a fourth part. Guadita (3) of my soul! Take good care of Teresita and your Carlitos, innocence is not regained. Any sacrifice is small and God will ask us an account of our children. Be sweet, amiable, self-denied, PATIENT, and have a great faith and confidence in God alone.

Infuse into your children a profound devotion to the Blessed Virgin. Receive the Sacraments frequently and be less worldly. Win Carlos (4) over through tenderness. May God bless you and may your home be a model of virtues. I expect you in heaven with all those you love and I say good-bye giving you my blessing.

(L.R., Vol. I/42)

---

(1) On September 11, she wrote in her *Spiritual Diary* (59/142) that she had high blood pressure and was in danger of a stroke. Feeling the peril of death, she wrote these recommendations and bits of advice to her daughter Lupe.

(2) Father Thomas Fallon, M.Sp.S., an Irishman who joined the Missionaries of the Holy Spirit, loved the Works of the Cross, and admired Mrs. Armida. He tried to help her even financially. He went to Ireland to try to obtain a loan for her sons in order to fortify their business.

(3) Nickname for Guadalupe.

(4) Carlos Lafarga y Aragón, husband of Guadalupe Armida y Cabrera (see data in letter 56).

To Her Brothers, Sisters, and In-Laws
From the Cabrera Line

Brothers and Sisters of
Concepción Cabrera De Armida

From the Christian marriage of Octaviano de Cabrera y Lacavex and Clara Arias y Rivera, twenty-one children were born, of whom only twelve survived.

1. MANUEL CABRERA Y ARIAS, who was married to Trinidad Ramos Flores, died tragically from an accidental gunshot wound on September 15, 1883, at the Hacienda of Jesús María S.L.P. leaving her a widow with three children: Manuel, Florencio, and María de la Luz.

2. OCTAVIANO CABRERA Y ARIAS married Carmen Hernández y de Ceballos. They had seven children: José, Octaviano, Carmen, Mercedes, Joaquín, Luz, and Jesús.

3. EMILIA CABRERA Y ARIAS married Doctor Ismael Salas. They were the parents of six children: Carlota, José Ismael, Emilia, Faustina, José de Jesús, and Clara.

4. JOSÉ CABRERA Y ARIAS died a bachelor in 1923.

5. LUIS CABRERA Y ARIAS married Carlota Wilson y Urquidi. This couple had five children: Carlota Matilde (who died at one year of age), Guadalupe, María de los Angeles, José Luis, and Carlota.

6. JUAN CABRERA Y ARIAS married Josefina Loustanau. They had five children: Carmen, Josefina, Guadalupe, Juan Manuel, and Primitivo.

7. CONCEPCIÓN CABRERA Y ARIAS (CONCHITA).

8. PRIMITIVO CABRERA Y ARIAS, born July 23, 1864, was a

Jesuit priest, for many years a missionary in the Tarahumara. He entered the Society of Jesus after the tragic accidental death of his brother Manuel, on March 29, 1892. In 1949, he died at 85 years of age in the Novitiate of San Cayetano, in the State of Mexico.

9. CLARA CABRERA Y ARIAS married Doctor Manuel Gallegos. They had only one daughter, Clarita, who died at the age of fifteen.

10. CARLOTA CABRERA Y ARIAS died at the age of three.

11. CONSTANTINO CABRERA Y ARIAS died eight days after his birth, on September 8, 1870.

12. FRANCISCO DE PAULA CABRERA Y ARIAS married Amparo Dávila y Ordorica. They had only three children: Francisco de Paula, Prisca, and Inocencia.

58

To Her Sister-in-Law Carlota Wilson

Jerusalem, October 21, 1913

My dear Carlitos (1):

Yesterday I received two letters from Pancho; they came together, the first I have received since I came here. I was longing for them. My heart told me that something had happened, and so it was! What a surprise to learn about the death of my beloved and unforgettable brother (2). May he rest in peace! You cannot imagine the terrible feeling we all experienced upon so suddenly reading about this great sorrow. My heart flew immediately to your side, a thousand memories crowded themselves in my heart, and with heart and soul I had wanted to be with you. God is so good. This sorrowful news reached me when I was making a day of retreat at Calvary. So there, in the hollow of the Cross, I left your sorrow and my own, and also the sorrow of your children, asking heaven for my dear brother and for you and for everyone perfect conformity with His Will.

The Lord knows what He is doing! Maybe the period of agony which lay before him would have made him suffer even more. That was his hour, it was the hour of his salvation so... let us thank God! Every day I wanted to write to you, but I did not want to miss a minute of the eight days we have spent in this so holy a land. As much as I could, I stayed at Calvary, in the Sepulcher, at the site where the Lord was nailed. Oh what things the Lord has let me see! Bethlehem, the Cenacle, Gethsemane, the Jordan, Jericho, the Mount of the Temptations, the many sites where He preached all the virtues through His example. Here every stone, every step, every person, object, or thing speaks about Jesus. I only missed my loved ones, that they might enjoy all this and their faith might be enlightened. You cannot imagine what one feels in these holy places. Of course one can feel the curse on this City in its dryness and ugliness. It grieves one to see the Holy Sepulcher, the Altar of the Crucifixion, the sepulcher of the Blessed Mother and the Cenacle in the hands of schismatics. In the Holy Sepulcher: Armenians, Turks, Greeks, and Catholics, each one in their turn. Bethlehem is charming. The Visitation is lovely; and so, for myself, since I entered Egypt, I have felt something else, reminiscences totally new and holy. All the pilgrims offered Communions, Masses and torrents of plenary indulgences which are granted at each site. And I, as much as I could, the same as Lupe and Nacho.

Carlitos of my soul, I do know what this sorrow is like, I would accompany you with a thousand hearts if I had them. When will I be able to embrace you? I have nothing and I am worth nothing, but you know that everything that is mine is also yours and with all my heart I will help in any way I can. Give me details, tell step by step about the illness and death of Luis, I want to know everything in detail. Send your letter to Rome, to the Pius Latin American Pontifical College, in care of Bishop Ibarra (3). I do not forget you and with a thousand embraces and kisses I say goodbye (4).

Concepción
(L.R., Vol. II/94-95)

(1) Familiar nickname for her sister-in-law Carlota Wilson, wife of her brother Luis Cabrera y Arias.

(2) Luis Cabrera y Arias, Mrs. Armida's fifth brother, was born in San Luis Potosí on November 29, 1856. He married Carlota Wilson y Urquidi, born on July 17, 1866. The wedding took place on January 8, 1886. They had

five children: Carlota Matilde died when she was a year old; Guadalupe Brígida, a Sister of the Sacred Heart; María de los Angeles; José Luis Gumersindo, a Jesuit priest; and Carlota, a Sister of the Sacred Heart.

(3) Ramón Ibarra y González, Archbishop of Puebla, who organized this pilgrimage to pray for Mexico during the revolution. He took Mrs. Armida to Rome so that the Holy Father St. Pius X could bless her and so that she could obtain permission and indulgences for the Works of the Cross, and particularly for the founding of the Missionaries of the Holy Spirit.

(4) Through this letter we can experience Mrs. Armida's sensitivity and her compassionate heart. The whole family really counted on her during all their troubles and times of need: to spend the night caring for the sick, to help them at the moment of their death, and to wrap them in their shroud; through her labor and her economic assistance, as far as her widowed condition could allow. Indeed, her sister-in-law Carlota soon after moved to Mexico City where she would find Concepción's companionship and support.

59

Baalbek, November 5, 1913

My dear Carlota:

I did not forget you yesterday, and I thought about you all day long, praying the Lord to console you and fill you with His blessings. Luis, already in the company of our dear beloved relatives who are awaiting us there, must have spent the day in heaven praying for you, for your children, and for me.

The Holy Land is done, and I left it with a deep sorrow; everything else has no attraction for me, except Rome. Calvary, Bethlehem, and Nazareth were the sites that moved me most; Saint John of the Mountain (the place of the Visitation), Mount Tabor, the whole of Galilee, Tiberias, Mount Carmel at Haifa, Mount Lebanon which we crossed, Damascus, where Saint Paul was converted; in sum, everything is so beautiful and full of holy memories. I have seen all the mysteries of the fifteenth hour (1); the Coronation in heaven is the only one I missed.

Baalbek is famous for its admirable ruins. One has to pay an entrance fee, but the Company (2) pays for everything: it is very convenient because they take care of the hotels, boats, luggage, rides, cars, wonderful dinners and even tips. Nevertheless there are people who are discontent, who complain. It makes one angry. As if with 1,700 pesos one, on his own, could have seen what we saw, always in first class with a doctor, thirty-one priests, an archbishop (3), and a bishop (4), staying with the Carmelites, the Franciscans; with interpreters, good four-wheeled carriages, etc. But one can find all sorts of persons in the vineyard of the Lord.

Beirut is a lovely port, and Port Said a resort. In the Palace

Hotel, where we are, we can see the ocean, the gardens and many steamers and boats from all over the world, and the Suez Canal. There are many Arabs, Turks, Africans, and Austrians. I, without leaving my room, have been on Spanish, Turkish, Austrian, and French ships. I see it and still cannot believe it. How I long to talk to you about the Holy Land! As soon as I get back, we shall get together for I hold you deep in my heart.

Tomorrow we will be in Alexandria, and from there to Brindisi, Naples, the ruins of Pompeii, Rome, Loreto, Padua, Assisi, Venice, Paris, Spain and... Mexico. Poor Mexico, here we only receive contradictory news.

To Carlotita (5) a thousand things. Show this letter to Pepe (6) and to Pancho (7). I wrote to them a few days ago; and with embraces to your children, I remain your sister who loves you so,

Concep.
(L.R., Vol. II/96–98)

(1) The Holy Rosary, with its fifteen mysteries.
(2) The Travel Agency "Wagon-Lits-Cook".
(3) His Excellency, Ramón Ibarra y González, Archbishop of Puebla, who led the trip.
(4) Bishop Amador. His Excellency, Archbishop Leopoldo Ruíz y Flores, had gone directly to Rome to prepare the way.
(5) Carlota Cabrera Wilson, later a religious of the Sacred Heart.
(6) José Cabrera y Arias, brother of Concepción, was born in San Luis Potosí. A poet, he never married.
(7) Francisco Cabrera y Arias, another brother of Concepción, was also born in San Luis Potosí. He was married to Amparo Dávila (see letters 61-64).

60

To Her Brother Primitivo Cabrera y Arias
Jesuit Priest
(Fragment)

August 9, 1904

My dear brother Primitivo:

...Look, pray the Lord that as long as He has bestowed so many graces upon me, He might crown them some day with the one of dying as a religious with Vows (1); this is my dream, my greatest ambition on earth. This may come as a surprise, but, in the end, I would be so happy if this were granted to me. I try to keep my neighbors' schedule (2) as much as I can, without neglecting my own obligations.

The Cross attracts me, the recollection, the Lord's presence, purity, the Tabernacle! That is where my life is! Always pure, always a victim! I repeat this to my dear Jesus of my soul a thousand times, to that Jesus Who is the treasure of my life.

So please answer me and do not play the duck as you did with the virtues; you already know that if I do not write to you it is not for lack of fondness or of desire to do so, but because of fear (3).

In Jesus; love Him, love Him and pray to Him for my children and for me. Encourage mamma (4) to receive Holy Communion often, okay?

(L.R., Vol. II/162)

(1) The desire to be a religious grew continuously throughout her life. She married without having met any religious, because they had been expelled from the country. Now she is a widow, but she must devote herself to her children. All the same, in 1929, when Salvador, her last son got married, she pleaded to Archbishop Luis María Martínez to permit her to enter the Congregation of the Sisters of the Cross of the Sacred Heart of Jesus. He did not consider this prudent. She experienced a great sorrow and cried bitterly. But on her trip to Rome in 1913, Bishop Ibarra, her spiritual director at the time, obtained from Pope Pius X that he would grant that she could make the religious vows at the hour of her death, and that she could live as a religious as far as it would be possible in her state in life.

(2) Mrs. Armida lived at 3 Mirto Street, and the Sisters of the Cross at 11 Mirto Street, next door.

(3) After Father Alberto Mir, S.J. disengaged himself from the Works of the Cross, the opinions of Jesuit priests were divided concerning Mrs. Armida and the Works of the Cross. So she, through prudence did not want to involve her brother, with whom she had special ties of fraternal affection, both because he was a priest and because they had grown up together, for he was the brother who came after her.

(4) Her mother, Clara Arias de Cabrera lived in Mexico City. A short time after this letter she died rather suddenly.

61

To Her Brother Francisco Cabrera y Arias

February 15

My dear brother Pancho:

I write to you with great difficulty because I am thoroughly exhausted. On the 21st, I will have been sick for three months, and after the capillary bronchopneumonia, its terrible consequences. And here I am full of fluid, soaked to the skin more than six times a day. Some blisters have burst, others punctured; I am afraid of gangrene. Whatever God wills.

Primitivo is in a place called Aguatempan, in the state of Puebla. I do not know when he will come. By the way, when is Amparo's operation? (1) I am worried; let me know the date so I can pray the Lord that she will come out all right; please tell her. I am with you and give her my regards. I almost cannot bear it, I do not sleep, I only take liquids, so I am very feeble.

With a thousand regards, your sister embraces you; and please tell the girls (2) to pray for me.

Concepción
(L.R., Vol. II/105-106)

(1) Amparo Dávila y Ordorica, wife of Francisco Cabrera y Arias.
(2) Maybe the daughters of her brother Octaviano: Carmen, Mercedes, and Luz Cabrera y Hernández.

62

April 9, 1936

My dear brother and sister Pancho and Amparo:

I have just received your letter, Pancho, in which you gave me the news of Panchito's death (1). I am so sorry for you and for his parents. He is the winner — a new little angel in heaven and an intercessor for all of us in that perpetual happiness which will have no end.

The circumstance of your not being in San Luis was terrible for everyone. It was God's will and you know I am near you in this just sorrow. May God grant that with such a terrible blow, María Luisa (2) will not have a relapse and become sick again.

I am going to advise my children (3) who will surely accompany you on this sad occasion. Salvador (4) is leaving on Sunday to visit his agent there and will continue on to Tampico, Torreón, Monterrey, etc. I am still ill, I cannot get better. So I am with you with all my love, my prayers, and thoughts. Your sister who embraces you.

Concepción
(L.R., Vol. IV/111)

---

(1) The grandchild of Francisco Cabrera y Arias and Amparo Dávila, and son of Francisco Cabrera y Dávila and María Luisa Sancha. He died as an infant.

(2) María Luisa Sancha, the mother of the deceased child.

(3) Conchita's children: Francisco, Ignacio, and Salvador, and her daughter Guadalupe.

(4) Salvador Armida y Cabrera. He went on business trips for the "Casa Armida", visiting the outlets they had in the different States of the Mexican Republic.

63

December 19, 1936

Cross (1)

My dear brother Pancho:

Here I am still in bed, when I would like to be singing the posadas, those of my mother that I used to sing every year with the grandchildren. Still with flu upon flu, and my liver does not want to reduce its swelling, and my cough does not let me sleep. I only take broth and I remember how delicious it was at your house; it is not possible for you to send me a small cup, is it? By the way, with this letter I send you and all your family my best wishes for Christmas and the New Year; may the Lord give them to you as I ask Him and wish them for you all. — December 23rd

I am only now able to continue albeit in my bed of suffering with a high fever, flu, liver condition, etc.. So these days are lovely to be born but not so to die. Whatever the Lord wills. Primitivo (2) is taking some vaccines for asthma. On the 25th he is going to give a retreat, I believe in San Juan del Río, and is coming back for the 1st. He has been well only when living with his own. He comes here daily.

So I wish a holy Christmas and New Year for you and for all your dear family, and I say good-bye with an embrace.

Concepción
(L.R., Vol. II/111)

---

(1) She begins using the word "Cross" in her letters: it is the period of her final "martyrdom."

(2) Fr. Primitivo, her Jesuit brother.

64

January 23, 1937

Cross

Mr. Francisco de P. Cabrera
P.O. Box 339
San Luis Potosí

My dear brother Pancho:

Having coming back from eternity, I am sending you these lines now that I can write somewhat. The trouble with my kidneys remains; I am swollen up to my waist, and also my heart... small things! Ask Amparo if she knows of anything that can take swelling down. I would even eat grasshopper's legs. Primitivo is going to Tacámbaro (1) and will go on a mission after that. So if God wills it, we shall see each other again.

Your sister embraces you and sends her regards to everyone. (2)

Concepción
(L.R., Vol. II/111)

(1) Tacámbaro is a small town in the state of Michoacán.
(2) This letter is possibly one of the last ones Mrs. Armida wrote, as she was to die on March 3rd. The last months of her life were very painful. She had complications in all of her vital organs, swollen legs with blisters and ulcers. Through this letter one can experience her care and concern for her loved ones. She writes with great difficulty.

To Her Brothers and Sisters In-Law
On the Armida Side

Brothers and Sisters In-Law on the Armida Side

Francisco Armida y García, husband of Concepción Cabrera y Arias, was, as we have already said, a son of Ildefonso Armida y Verdejo and of Petra García y Delgado. They had nine children:

ROSARIO, who married Manuel Viadero in 1871. She had ten girls: Emilia, Carmen, Josefina, Manuela, María, Amalia, Dolores, Rosario, Felipa and Margarita. Her second marriage was to Leopoldo Viadero, a brother of her former husband; they had two boys: Manuel and Leopoldo.

ANTONIO, who married Emilia Cartensen. They had three girls: María, Teresa (Techa) and Belén, a widow of Mr. Espinoza. They also had a son, Antonio (?).

ILDEFONSO, who married Damiana Torres on July 24, 1894. They had five children: José, who married; María Luisa, single; Rosa, a Sister of the Cross of the Sacred Heart of Jesus; Enrique, who married; and Guadalupe, also a Sister of the Cross.

FRANCISCO, Conchita's husband.

DOLORES, who married Fernando Manrique de Lara on January 10, 1885. They had three children: Guillermo, Roberto and María.

PETRA, who married Eugenio Ortiz in 1887. They had no children.

EUGENIO, who died at birth.

JOSÉ, who married Eloísa Sada in Saltillo on July 27, 1887.

CARMEN, the youngest, married Eugenio Ortiz.

65

To Her Sister-in-Law Rosario Armida De Viadero

Mexico City, July 11, 1913
Mrs. Rosario A. de Viadero
San Luis Potosí

My dear sister:

Today it is fifteen days since the blessed death of Pablo (1) and with such a blow and the normal upset of nine days of mourning, I am now experiencing terrible exhaustion. I can hardly lift my head and my pulse still trembles. In a postcard I asked Pepe (2) to inform you, for I was alone and without servants (because one of them had a terrible case of erysipelas and even received the last Sacraments here in the house and the other one was taking care of her). I only had the cook. What a blow to the middle of the heart! But if we see things from faith's point of view, how happy I am to already have three in heaven (3) well insured, and two in the heaven on earth, that is in religious life (4).

A few months back Pablo was telling me that he wanted to die, and after supper, two or three days before becoming ill, he told me: "Mommy, you will have a dead person here pretty soon." This, even though I did not let him see my amazement, impressed me, and when he fell ill, I foresaw that from this severe illness he would leave me for heaven. With a great fervor he asked for the Viaticum and all the aids of our religion and even the Third Order of Saint Francis. He made many acts of love, repeatedly accepting his sufferings and death. He often caressed the Crucifix saying only: "My Lord, Your Will, not mine, be done."

You cannot imagine how greatly we have been affected. He was a model son, extremely humble, self-denied, and given to the service of others. But God does everything perfectly. He only took what already was His. Blessed be God! Do not forget him and myself in your prayers. Salvador and Lupe found him already gone. Poor things! Salvador has left and Lupe we shall see. And Elisa (5) lost her mother four days ago (6). My regards to the girls (7). I am sorry for you because of the lack of communication with Leopoldo (8) and with your sons (9). God wills it! Your sister who loves you greatly embraces you.

Concepción
(L.R., Vol. II/42-44)

(1) Pablo Armida y Cabrera, the seventh son of Francisco Armida y García and Concepción Cabrera y Arias. He was born on June 19, 1896, and died on June 27, 1913, in Mexico City.

(2) Her brother José Cabrera y Arias, who lived in San Luis Potosí.

(3) Three of her sons. Carlos Armida y Cabrera, her second child, was born on March 28 and baptized on April 3, 1887. He died at six years of age on March 10, 1893, in San Luis Potosí. She recalls that when the death of this son occurred, her husband was in bad economic circumstances and had to take out a loan to pay for the burial of her little boy. Pedro Armida y Cabrera, the youngest of her children, was born on February 20, 1899, and died on April 7, 1902. This was one of the greatest sorrows Mrs. Armida experienced: she had become a widow on September 17, 1901, and Francisco had asked her to take special care of this youngest son. He drowned accidentally in the fountain of their house. And now she has lost her son Pablo, seventeen years old.

(4) Her religious children. Manuel Armida y Cabrera was in Spain with the Jesuits. Concepción (Teresa de María in religious life) entered the Sisters of the Cross of the Sacred Heart of Jesus, where she died on December 19, 1925.

(5) Elisa Baz y Duclaud, wife of her son Francisco Armida y Cabrera.

(6) Mrs. Bertha Duclaud de Baz.

(7) Rosario Armida y García married Manuel Viadero and they had ten girls.

(8) Her second marriage was to Leopoldo Viadero, a brother of her former husband with whom she had two sons. Their lack of communication is possibly due to the revolution in the Mexican Republic.

(9) Manuel and Leopoldo Viadero y Armida.

66

Mexico City, April 5, 1914
Mrs. Rosario A. de Viadero
San Luis Potosí

My dear sister:

I have been wanting to write to you every day, but it was impossible. After so much sea, I arrived ill, and after I got up, I started to fix everything up so as to profit from the benefit of the Grace granted to me in Rome, the one of having the Blessed Sacrament in my home. Just imagine what a joy! After this I only desire heaven. I burst with happiness and now you have me here enjoying such a lovely Guest since the 25th. See when you can come to visit Him.

What an unforgettable trip to Jerusalem and Rome! I do not know how to thank the Lord for it. How anxious I am to tell you about everything I saw! So many marvels of our beloved religion. Bethlehem, Nazareth, Jericho, the Dead Sea, the Jordan, Lazarus' tomb, Mount Tabor, Calvary, the Stone of the Anointing, the Holy Sepulcher, Emmaus, the Mount of Olives with the footprints of the Lord, and also the Quo Vadis in Rome. A piece of His cross, the thorns of the crown, the column of the flagellation, the Cenacle, Mount Carmel, we drank water from the well of the Samaritan woman, Tiberiades, Capernaum, Bethany, and also Damascus, Baalbek, Mount Lebanon, Beirut, and six or seven cities in Italy.

In Spain I saw Manuel (1); he sends you his regards, he is very advanced in his spirituality and in his studies. I was not able to see Emilia (2); we stayed too far away. We were in San Sebastián, Loyola, Cestoria, Barcelona, Valencia, Málaga, and Cádiz. I did not forget you in those holy places. I will send you some relics. Did you know about my brother Luis (3) who died? Who could have told me I would never see him again!

Carlota (4) came night before last and is looking for a house near to me. I hope she finds it! Pancho (5) is in New York settling some business. If what he now has in sight does come through, the first ones who will profit from it will be the family and the first ones among them, it is clear, will be all of you. Pray the Lord. And Antonio? (6) Is he still in the Peñasco? Until I am able to write to him, say hello to him and his family. To all your girls, a thousand regards, and to Leopoldo when you write to him, and to the boys. Regards also from Nacho and Lupe and you well know how much your sister loves you.

Concepción
(L.R., Vol. II/46–48)

---

(1) Her religious son Manuel Armida y Cabrera (see letters 4-24).
(2) Possibly Emilia Viadero y Armida, daughter of Rosario Armida y García and Manuel Viadero.
(3) Luis Cabrera y Arias, who died while Mrs. Armida was on her trip to the Holy Land.
(4) The widow of Luis Cabrera y Arias, Carlota Wilson y Urquidi.
(5) Francisco Armida y Cabrera.
(6) Antonio Armida y García.

67

To Her Brother-in-Law Antonio Armida y García

April 20, 1908

My dear brother and sister, Antonio and Emilia:

Concha (1) left me this letter for you and so you will learn about the sorrowful moment I am going through (2). God willed it. She gave it much thought and consulted on the matter and so did I; she went of her free will and choice, and I blessed her a thousand times in her father's name and in my own name. On Friday at three o'clock I made the sacrifice: I took her and delivered her there, and yesterday, the nineteenth at 8:30 in the morning she began her religious life. She is very happy; she was too pure a soul to remain in the world, and the Lord chose her like a lily for his garden. Together with your girls, help me to thank God for such a great gift!

So, if my motherly heart does suffer and bleed, my Christian faith and my duty tell me that I must sacrifice any natural feeling before the voice of God and His holy Will. Octaviano (3) came to hand her over. Pancho has behaved as a model Christian. The farewells, the blessings etc. were very very painful, but blessed be the Lord for everything. How is Antonio feeling?

Please send this enclosed letter to Soledad, I do not know the address and do not want it to be lost.

With regards to the three little nephews and pray for Concha and for myself; You can read the letters for Carmen (4).

Concepción
(L.R., Vol. II/166-167)

(1) Concepción Armida y Cabrera.

(2) The entrance into religious life of this daughter, who received the name of Teresa de María Inmaculada, with the Sisters of the Cross of the Sacred Heart of Jesus (see letters 25 to 36).

(3) Octaviano Cabrera y Arias, brother of Concepción, who was like a father to her children when she became the widow of Francisco Armida y García.

(4) Carmen Armida y García, who was married to Mr. Eugenio Ortíz.

68

To Her Sister-in-Law Emilia Cartensen De Armida

Mexico City, September 16, 1916
Mrs. Emilia C. de Armida
San Luis

My dear Emilia:

You can imagine the surprise I had upon learning from your telegram of Antonio's death (1), without having had any prior notice of his serious illness. We have felt it deeply and have thought about you and your children in such terrible sorrow. Fernando (2) told Pancho that he had caught a sort of pneumonia. I knew he had trouble with his larynx.

It has been God's will, my dear little sister, and I ask Him to console you and to be your spouse now and always. I had not written to you because I had been ill with some renal trouble, a cerebral anemia and exhaustion. It is only natural that we are going downhill. As long as we arrive in heaven, everything is good. So my deepest condolences to you, your girls and your son, and as soon as I am able to do it, I will write to the girls (3). Become saintly and you know, even though my prayers are not worth much, Masses, etc. here in my small chapel have been offered for this beloved soul.

You know how much your sister loves you and is with you from the bottom of her heart.

Concepción
(L.R., Vol. II/168-169)

(1) Antonio Armida y García.

(2) A relative or a partner in the Casa Armida.

(3) Possibly the other sisters Armida y García: Rosario, Dolores, Petra and Carmen.

69

San Angel
November 4, 1922
Mrs. Emilia C. de Armida
San Luis

My dear little sister:

Thank you a thousand times for your congratulations for my great happiness: Manuel (1), a priest! (2) What can a mother desire that can be greater than this? Please help me to thank the Lord for this immense and unmerited gift! I also thank you for your condolences for our adorable Nachito (3). How quickly he flew up to heaven! His parents (4) are unconsolable, and I, also, have felt it deeply. Nacho and Chabela left for Europe on the 30th; Nacho had to go to Germany and hopes Chabela will be distracted. She is three and a half months along with another child, and we hope to God she returns without incident; please pray for this intention.

I am sorry for the liver illness that has overtaken you. Take care of yourself and also Tere (5). I am sorry about your illness, if the Lord wills it may He give you prompt relief.

My regards to María (6), Techa (7) and to Belén (8) and her husband (9), to the Viaderos (10) a thousand sweet things. Lupe says hello to everybody and I send you all a tight embrace.

Concepción
(L.R., Vol. II/168-169)

---

(1) Manuel Armida y Cabrera, a Jesuit priest, was ordained in Barcelona on July 31, 1922.

(2) Mrs. Armida appreciated as a mother and as a Christian the grace to have a son as a priest. Her spiritual mission was especially dedicated to them

and it must have been a great joy for her that a son of hers received that favor. Her spiritual happiness was again marked with the cross; she renewed her sacrifice of not seeing him and not assisting at his ordination.

(3) Her grandson Ignacio Armida y Morán.

(4) Ignacio Armida y Cabrera and his wife Isabel Morán y Bolaños Cacho. Their little son died on October 12, 1922.

(5) Her daughter, Teresa.

(6) María Armida y Cartensen.

(7) Teresa Armida y Cartensen.

(8) Belén Armida y Cartensen de Espinoza.

(9) Mr. Espinoza.

(10) The daughters of Rosario Armida and Manuel Viadero.

70

Mexico City
May 24, 1933
Mrs. Emilia C. Armida
San Luis Potosí

My dear Emilia:

You cannot imagine what a sorrowful surprise it was for me when I read your card upon arriving here from León on Monday, the 22nd. Techa was my angel and with her life full of suffering, she will surely be in heaven praying for us. Looking at things in a purely human way, together with all my children, I give you and María and Belén my condolences, but on the divine side, I congratulate you for having that angel in heaven. I did not know anything of her grave illness.

Since the beginning of March, I went to Morelia (1) and then to León (2). There I was ill and came back to Mexico City until two days ago, as I told you. Let us adore God's will! Happy are we for having faith and do not cry without hope! It will not be long before we go to join our loved ones! The sorrows of life will seem as nothing in that joyful eternity. Blessed be God for everything! And your health, did it get worse? And that of María?

As soon as my health is better I want to go to San Luis, and I will have the pleasure of embracing you.

I am now writing to you from my bed; the fever will not leave me, and so I must close now, I am very weak. A big hug for María and another one for you from your sister who loves you much. Think that everything passes away except having suffered for God with love.

Concepción
(L.R., Vol. II/180–182)

(1) She had gone to make her yearly retreat under the guidance of Archbishop Martínez.

(2) Coming back from Morelia to Mexico City she used to stop in León to rest and then, because of her heart trouble, slowly progress to the higher altitude. The Madrigal family had invited her and she also took advantage of visiting the Sisters of the Cross, who had a House there.

To Her Grandchildren

Her Grandchildren

The oldest grandchildren were the two children of FRANCISCO ARMIDA Y CABRERA and Elisa Baz Duclaud:

FRANCISCO ARMIDA Y BAZ, was born on April 15, 1917, and married Beda Muñoz y Castillo on April 14, 1945. Their children, great-grandchildren of Mrs. Armida, were: María Concepción Armida y Muñoz, who married Jorge Soto Mayor y Canales; Beda, who died as a little girl; Francisco Manuel Armida y Muñoz, who married Silvia Magali y Gallardo Meza; and Alejandro José Armida y Muñoz.

MARIA CECILIA ARMIDA Y BAZ, was born in Mexico City on March 6, 1921. She married Leendert van Rhijn on November 26, 1945. They had an only child, Patricia Guadalupe van Rhijn, who married Antonio Castellanos on March 1, 1968; they had two children, great-great-grandchildren of Mrs. Armida: Federico Castellanos y van Rhijn and Elisa Castellanos y van Rhijn.

IGNACIO ARMIDA Y CABRERA and Isabel Morán y Bolaños Cacho gave birth to nine children:

JOSÉ IGNACIO ARMIDA Y MORÁN, born on June 25, 1920, and died on the same day.

IGNACIO ARMIDA Y MORÁN, born on June 20, 1921, and died on October 17, 1922.

MANUEL ARMIDA Y MORÁN, born in Mexico City on March 30, 1923, married María de la Luz León de la Barra, who was born in Mexico City on December 30, 1925. The wedding took place on

July 26, 1947. Manuel died on May 29, 1953 in an automobile accident. He left two children: Isabel Armida y León de la Barra, born on May 2, 1948. On December 22, 1972, she married Marcelo Roseto and had a daughter, Isabel Roseto y Armida, born on November 8, 1973 (great-great-grandchild of Mrs. Armida). The other child of Manuel Armida y Morán was Manuel Armida y León de la Barra, still a bachelor.

IGNACIO ARMIDA Y MORÁN, born in Mexico City on January 16, 1925, married María Graham y Soberón, who was born on December 3, 1928, also in Mexico City. They had seven children: María Guadalupe, Ignacio, Xavier, Pablo, Juan Luis, Tomás and Andrés, great-grandchildren of Mrs. Armida.

CARLOS ARMIDA Y MORÁN was born on December 8, 1927, and married Margarita Obregón y Zetina on February 8, 1956. They had seven children: Carlos Gustavo, Margarita, Consuelo, María Eugenia, Gabriela, Gustavo, and José Luis Armida y Obregón, great-grandchildren of Mrs. Armida.

CONCEPCIÓN ARMIDA Y MORÁN was born on June 12, 1930, and married Manuel Mier y Terán y del Valle on April 14, 1956. They had seven children: Manuel Ignacio, Mauricio, Alejandro, María Isabel, Juan Pablo, Carlos, and Concepción Mier y Terán y Armida, great-grandchildren of Mrs. Armida.

JACOBO ARMIDA Y MORÁN was born on April 14, 1932, and married Inés Verea y Campos, who was born on November 29, 1936; the wedding took place on May 22, 1958. They had five children: Inés, Santiago, Anna Paula, Fernando José, and Diego Antonio Armida y Verea, great-grandchildren of Mrs. Armida.

ISABEL ARMIDA Y MORÁN, was born on September 14, 1934, and married Federico Mantilla y Montiel, who was born on January 17, 1925. Their children are: Federico, Gerardo, and Isabel Mantilla y Armida, great-grandchildren of Mrs. Armida.

GUILLERMO ARMIDA Y MORÁN, born on June 8, 1936. He married Luisa Noriega y García Ruíz. The wedding took place on May 2, 1962. Their children are: Guillermo, Juan Felipe, Pedro Pablo, and Luisa Armida y Noriega, great-grandchildren of Mrs. Armida.

CONSUELO ARMIDA Y MORÁN, entered the convent of the Sisters of the Sacred Heart.

GUADALUPE ARMIDA Y CABRERA was born on February 11, 1898 in San Luis Potosí and on May 15, 1924 she married Carlos Lafarga y Aragón who was born in the month of March 1893. They had two children:

MARIA TERESA LAFARGA Y ARMIDA was born on April 9, 1925, and married Constantino Madero y González. He was born on May 25, 1916, and died on September 27, 1947, leaving her a widow with two children: María Teresa Madero y Lafarga, born on December 15, 1946, married Diego Fernando Flores Hurtado on May 8, 1965. They have three children: Diego Antonio, Alejandro, and Paola Flores y Madero, great-great-grandchildren of Mrs. Armida.

CARLOS LAFARGA Y ARMIDA was born on June 16, 1932. He married María de la Luz González y Rojo Matute on June 18, 1955. They have three children, great-grandchildren of Mrs. Armida: Carlos, Francisco Xavier, and María de la Luz Lafarga y González.

Only Francisco, Ignacio, and Guadalupe had children.

Manuel became a Jesuit priest; Concepción was a Sister of the Cross; Carlos died when he was six years old, Pedro at three, and Pablo at sixteen. Salvador had no children.

71

To Her Grandchild Manuel Armida y Morán

January 2, 1936

My dear little son Meme:

I ask the Lord to give you a very holy year full of satisfaction. I think we will be seeing each other pretty soon because your father (1) says you will be coming in the middle of the month. I hope you will be able to enter school with the Brothers of San Borja (2). What about Christmas? Here the tree is very beautiful and we missed you a lot during the posadas. Regards to everybody and your Mane (3) blesses you.

Concepción
(L.R., Vol. I/70)

(1) Ignacio Armida y Cabrera.
(2) The Brothers of the Christian Schools who had their school on Avenida San Borja, between Colonia del Valle and Coyoacán. During the religious persecution in Mexico, children had to keep up their studies undercover in houses, so as not to receive the atheist education. Eventually, this magnificent school was taken over by the government and converted into a public school.
(3) "Mane" is short for "mamá grande." Her grandchildren called her thus.

72

To Her Grandchild Ignacio Armida y Morán

January 2, 1936

My dear son Nachito:

I wish you a happy New Year with all my heart. May the Child Jesus fill you with His graces so you may be a model and an example for your little brothers and sisters. Here we had the posadas with singing, a procession, a tree, etc. We really missed you all. I hope to see you soon, and in the meantime I send you a hug.

Your Mane.
Concepción
(L.R., Vol. I/69)

To Her Nephews and Nieces,
Cabrera Family

Nieces and nephews who appear in these letters

OCTAVIANO LIBORIO CABRERA Y HERNÁNDEZ, son of Octaviano Cabrera y Arias, brother of Concepción, and of Carmen Hernández y Ceballos. He was born in San Luis Potosí on July 23, 1879. A civil engineer, he embellished his native city with buildings of neoclassic style with pink stone facades. He married Matilde Anna Ipiña de Verástegui on January 18, 1906. They had seven children: Matilde, Octaviano, Carmen, Elena, María Luisa, Ernesto, and Bertha.

CLARA SALAS Y CABRERA, daughter of Emilia Cabrera y Arias, sister of Concepción, born in San Luis Potosí on October 8, 1852, and of Ismael Salas, who were married on July 20, 1869. Clara was born in San Luis Potosí on April 12, 1892, and married José Perogordo y Lasso de la Vega on May 14, 1914. They had five children, all of them born in San Luis Potosí: Guadalupe, José, Clara Elena, Carlos, and Martha.

FAUSTINA SALAS Y CABRERA, sister of Clara, was born in San Luis Potosí on March 22, 1880. She entered the Society of the Sacred Heart, where she made her religious vows in 1907.

DOCTOR JOAQUÍN CABRERA Y LÓPEZ, a grandson of Octaviano Cabrera y Arias, the brother of Concepción, and son of Joaquín Cabrera Hernández and his first wife, Guadalupe López Hermosa. When his first wife died, Octaviano married his deceased wife's sister, Angela, whom the doctor and his brothers and sisters considered their second mother.

CARMEN RIVERO Y CABRERA DE CABALLERO, was born on May

26, 1911. She married Roberto Caballero on January 12, 1933. They had no children. She was a daughter of Mercedes Cabrera y Hernández — daughter of Octaviano Cabrera y Arias and Carmen Hernández y Ceballos — and of Angel Rivero Caloca of Mexico City. The wedding took place on October 12, 1908, in the Temple of San Agustín in the capital city of San Luis Potosí.

LUIS CABRERA Y WILSON, son of Luis Cabrera y Arias — brother of Concepción — and of Carlota Wilson y Urquidi. He was born on January 13, 1898, in San Luis Potosí. He entered the Society of Jesus on May 2, 1923, and was ordained a priest on August 25, 1936. He died on January 26, 1985.

CARLOTA CABRERA Y WILSON, sister of Luis, was born on July 13, 1901, in San Luis Potosí. She entered the Society of the Sacred Heart on January 7, 1922 and was the Provincial of the Mexican Province when she died tragically in an automobile accident on December 19, 1964, while on her way to the ground-breaking of the Sacred Heart School in Guadalajara, Jalisco.

IGNACIO MURIEL Y CABRERA, was born in San Luis Potosí on October 12, 1883. Grandson of Florencio Cabrera and Manuela Otahegui. His parents were: María de Jesús Cabrera y Otahegui and Ignacio Muriel y Soberón. He married Guadalupe de la Meza y de Icaza and they had two children, Ignacio and Guadalupe.

LUZ CABRERA Y HERNÁNDEZ, daughter of Octaviano Cabrera y Arias — brother of Concepción — married Arturo Marti y de los Heros on June 12, 1906. They had nine children. The seventh one was Carmen, born on March 18, 1920. She died as an infant and is the one mentioned in letter 84. Arturo and Ramón were the first and third of the children, respectively. Luz Cabrera y Hernández was born in San Luis Potosí on May 23, 1888, and Arturo was born on October 29, 1879.

73

To Her Nephew Octaviano L. Cabrera y Hernández

Mexico City, January 12, 1906
Mr. Octaviano L. Cabrera
San Luis Potosí

My dearest Tano:

First through Octaviano (1) and afterward through your letter, I learned that your happiness (2) would be delayed until the 18th. It is not so long even though it may seem so to you; patience. I'm sure it was so that Matilde (3) could finish taking care of her face or teeth; they told me she had been very swollen. Is she better? Ana (4) asks me to give her regards to the Engineer (5) of the Cross, who graduated on that Feast Day, and to tell you that on the 18th they all (6) will be praying for the happiness of the new couple. To your father (7), mother (8) and girls (9) along with Joaquín (10) and Jesús (11) my loving regards, and also to my future niece, and to you; receive a warm embrace from your aunt, who you well know loves you.

Concepción

I have had Lupe in bed with intestinal trouble, but thank God, she is better.

(L.R., Vol. II/138-139)

---

(1) Octaviano Cabrera y Arias, brother of Conchita.
(2) His planned wedding.

(3) Matilde Anna Ypiña de Verástegui, daughter of José María de la Encarnación Ypiña y de la Peña and Luisa de Verástegui y Ruiz de Bustamante. She was born on February 10, 1881. They had seven children: Matilde, Octaviano, Carmen, Elena, María Luisa, Ernesto and Berta.

(4) Ana Apolonia Cabrera y Otahegui, daughter of Florencio de Cabrera y Lacavex and Manuela Otahegui. She was Superior General of the Sisters of the Cross of the Sacred Heart of Jesus, and a relative of Octaviano.

(5) Engineer Octaviano Liborio Cabrera y Hernández, himself.

(6) The Sisters of the Cross of the Sacred Heart of Jesus.

(7) Octaviano Cabrera y Arias.

(8) Carmen Hernández y Ceballos.

(9) The daughters of Octaviano and Carmen Hernández: Carmen, Mercedes, and Luz Cabrera y Hernández.

(10) Joaquín Cabrera y Hernández was born on September 22, 1886. He first married Doña Guadalupe López Hermosa with whom he had three children: Joaquín, Guadalupe, and Clara. When he became a widower, he married the sister of his former wife, Angela López Hermosa, with whom he had six children: Octaviano, María de Lourdes, Concepción, Enrique, Salvador, and Manuel Cabrera López.

(11) Jesús Cabrera y Hernández, who married Rebeca Sánchez. When she died, he married Guadalupe Gordoa y Dumbar. They had three children: María Martha, María Teresa, and Jesús José Antonio Cabrera y Gordoa.

74

To Her Niece Clara Salas y Cabrera

Mexico City, May 8, 1902

My dearest Clarita:

What a day! The happiest one in your life! Blessed be God who grants it to you, to fill your soul with His graces. Your father (1) must be full of joy today and maybe the Blessed Virgin will obtain for you the grace of a vocation, like Carlota (2). I accompany you with all my heart from here, and Concha (3) has not forgotten you for a moment. Won't you please send us a picture; we are eager to see you just as you are. Your mother (4) and Carlota most especially must have experienced a great happiness in seeing Our Lord come to your heart for the first time. Your aunt loves you greatly and sends your mother and sisters (5) my heartiest congratulations.

Concepción
(L.R., Vol. II/211-212)

(1) Ismael Salas.
(2) Carlota Salas y Cabrera, born on September 4, 1873. She entered a religious order on December 24, 1901, and died in 1936.
(3) Concepción Armida y Cabrera.
(4) Emilia Cabrera y Arias de Salas, sister of Concepción.
(5) Emilia, and Faustina Salas y Cabrera.

75

Mexico City, May 11, 1914
Miss Clara Salas
Querétaro

My dearest Claris:

I really appreciated the invitation to your wedding, but you see it is impossible for Brígida (1) to go. I wanted to send Lupe with Pancho, who was going to go, but Elisa (2) came back sick and it is not possible for her to go either. She is all swollen up and they sent her to have an analysis made. We do not know the results, but she is really in bad condition. Pancho is alarmed and we hope to God this will not be serious.

So you are going to get married tomorrow! God provides things sometimes where and when one least imagines! You know how heartily I have always loved you and how much I want you to be happy: a model spouse, and example of virtue who leads many souls to heaven.

It truly upsets me not to be able to see you, would it be only through a little hole, on that joyful day. God wills it! Mass, Communion, and everything tomorrow for the couple, a dear niece and nephew (3). At least you were able to be with the family and acquaintances from Potosí.

Will you not be coming here for at least a week? What a pleasure it would be to embrace the new couple. I sent you a little present by express, a jewelry box that you will use remembering me.

To Octa (4) a thousand things, that I will write soon. Give my loving and best wishes to José (5), and receive a thousand congratulations and the embraces from your old aunt who loves you so much.

Concepción
(L.R., Vol. II/213-214)

(1) Maybe Brígida Pérez Palacios, mother of Luis Alcorta and of Mother Dolores Alcorta. They lived near Mrs. Armida and the Sisters of the Cross in Colonia Santa María.

(2) Elisa Baz y Duclaud, wife of Francisco Armida y Cabrera.

(3) Clara Salas y José Perogordo.

(4) Octaviano Cabrera y Arias.

(5) José Perogordo, Clarita's husband.

76

To Mr. José Perogordo
Husband of Clara Salas y Cabrera

Mexico City, San Angel
November 7, 1924
Don José Perogordo, Attorney
San Luis Potosí

My dear compadre (1):

I am going to give you some trouble, and please forgive me. Elisa really liked the poncho that I brought to Chabela from the factory, and I would very much appreciate it if you could do me the favor of sending another one to me, or have one sent. I hope that the bands along the border are not blue but another color, perhaps yellow. I would also like to know the price of the scarves and if you have them in stock, and also if you might have some "defective ones" (I do not remember how they refer to them). Have the factory send me an order form so that I can ask for them directly and not bother you. How is Claris (2)? When?… Let us see if she has another little boy. A thousand regards from me and when you see Pancho (3) and Juanita (4), the same to them.

To the children, my love, and for you an embrace from your old aunt and "comadre" who loves you dearly.

Concepción

Meche (5) will send you 12.50 pesos on my behalf for the poncho;

that is what the one I brought with me cost, but if it is more, please let me know.

2 De la Paz Ave., San Angel, Mexico City

(L.R., Vol. II/204)

(1) In Mexico, relationship between the godfather and the parents of the child. José Perogordo was the lawyer for a textile factory and "compadre" of Concepción, and she was the "comadre."

(2) Clara Salas y Cabrera, niece of Mrs. Armida and wife of José Perogordo.

(3) Francisco Sandoval Navarro.

(4) Juanita Bárcenas de Sandoval. A married woman. She and her husband were friends of José Perogordo. They knew and admired Concepción.

(5) Mercedes Cabrera y Hernández de Rivero, daughter of Octaviano.

To Sister Faustina Salas y Cabrera

Mexico City, Coyoacán
February 15, 1935

My dear Mother Faustina (Faustina Salas y Cabrera, religious of the Sacred Heart):

Today is your saint's day, and I do not want it to pass without congratulating you. I learned you are ill and I am so sorry, but you well know that sorrow unites us to the Lord. May He give you patience and a great reward in heaven. Here we are suffering from many things. Emilia (1) with a heart condition and Ramón (2) is very old. Young Emilia (3) has three cute boys and a little girl, as you must know. Lupe (4) is in Monterrey; who knows if they will close their school.

I have been quite ill with my heart condition, and I took a terrible fall. I had a brain concussion and spent several days in bed. Your family who lives here has had many sorrows and hardships. Primitivo is (5) in Mérida and Manuel (6) in Brussels. Luis Cabrera (7) is going to be ordained there in Belgium; he is near Manuel in another school. You can see, so much news. The one essential thing is to become holy, here below everything passes, except having suffered for the Lord with love. Oh! Love is everything! Pray the Lord I do not stop loving Him even for a moment, that every moment I may do His will, however painful it may be. I believe I will die soon; it is about time and I have fulfilled my mission here on earth. May He forgive my innumerable shortcomings, so many! Ask Him to deal with me however He pleases; I am His own without conditions, even though I may be rubbish.

Do you have the book *Jesus, What Is He Really Like?* Do not forget me in your prayers; take me out of purgatory and I say goodbye with an embrace.

Your aunt,
Concepción
(L.R., Vol. II/188-190)

(1) Emilia Salas y Cabrera, born in San Luis Potosí on March 14, 1878. Daughter of Emilia Cabrera y Arias and of Ismael Salas, sister of Mother Faustina.

(2) Ramón Rivero y Soberón, husband of Emilia, born on August 9, 1860. Their wedding took place on August 12, 1904. They had twin daughters: Guadalupe and Emilia.

(3) Emilia Rivero y Salas, born on January 24, 1908. She married Aniceto Ortega y Espinosa on July 29, 1931. They had one daughter, Teresa, and three sons: Aniceto, Carlos, and Salvador. Afterward, another seven, Javier, Ramón, Alejandro, Emilia, María de la Paz, Guadalupe, and José Antonio Ortega y Rivero.

(4) Guadalupe Rivero y Salas, sister of Emilia and niece of Mother Faustina, born on January 24, 1909. She entered the Society of the Sacred Heart on February 26, 1929.

(5) Father Primitivo Cabrera y Arias, S.J., missionary.

(6) Manuel Armida y Cabrera, S.J., son of Mrs. Armida, expelled from Spain because of the civil and religious war.

(7) Father Luis Cabrera y Wilson, S.J. son of Luis Cabrera y Arias and Carlota Wilson. His father died while Mrs. Armida was on her trip to the Holy Land and Rome (see letters 58, 59).

78

To Her Nephew Joaquín Cabrera y López

August 16, 1936
Mr. Joaquín Cabrera

My dear Joaquín:

Today is your saint's day; I have not forgotten you before the Lord, nor have I forgotten your father (1) God rest his soul. May the Lord bless you and help you to finish your studies (2) so you can do much good in the world. I do not know if my congratulations are going to reach you today as the post office does not deliver on Sundays, but the Lord knows how much I have been thinking about you today. My regards to Angela (3) and to your brothers and sisters (4) and your old aunt embraces you.

Concepción
(L.R., Vol. II/128)

---

(1) Joaquín Cabrera y Hernández, son of Octaviano Cabrera y Arias and of Carmen Hernández de Ceballos. He first married Guadalupe López Hermosa and had three children: Joaquín, Guadalupe, and Clara. In his second marriage to Angela, the sister of his former wife, he had six children: Octaviano, María de Lourdes, Concepción, Enrique, Salvador, and Manuel.

(2) He studied medicine, specializing in orthopedics and was director of the railroad hospital. He practiced his profession with great skill and Christian charity. He married Elisa Camargo, who preceded him in death. He died on October 30, 1988.

(3) Angela López Hermosa, sister of his mother and a true mother to them.

(4) His sisters, Guadalupe and Clara, and the brothers and sisters of his father's second marriage.

79

To Her Niece
Carmen Rivero y Cabrera De Caballero

August 8, 1933

My dear Carmelita:

Along with Primitivo I am sending you a small gift, but one full of love; the crisis does not allow me to do more. I would love to see you as a bride, but send me your picture, you must be gorgeous. May the Lord bless the lovely couple. On the 12th, I will be praying for you that you may form a Christian home. Truly, Carmela (1), I wish you all sorts of happiness. We presume the wedding will take place at the Asylum (2) because of the mourning. You will let me know where your house is. A thousand regards to your mother, to Meche (3) and Gelo (4), to Octa, and especially to Roberto (5); let him have this letter as if it were his own, and may the Lord bestow His blessings on you both. Your aunt, who loves you dearly, embraces you.

Concepción
(L.R., Vol. II/217)

(1) Carmen Rivero y Cabrera was a daughter of Mercedes Cabrera y Hernández de Ceballos (daughter of Octaviano Cabrera y Arias and of Carmen Hernández de Ceballos) and of Angel Rivero y Caloca.
(2) The Asylum Gabriel Aguirre, administrated by Octaviano.
(3) Mercedes Rivero y Cabrera — sister of Carmelita — married Juan Pons y Zenteno.
(4) Angel Rivero y Cabrera — brother of Carmelita — married Amalia López y Viadero.
(5) Roberto Caballero, the husband of Carmelita. They had no children.

80

For Carmen Rivero

CONSOMME
3/4 kg of tenderloin
2 carrots
2 tomatoes
one or two eggs
a little celery
two stems of parsley
Pepper. Onions. Salt.

Ask for fresh meat and chop it, fry it in a little bit of lard. Once fried, put in the sliced tomatoes and the chopped carrots. You add the two beaten raw eggs, the parsley, etc. Let it boil in two liters of water for three hours. Strain it through a napkin and add a bit of burnt sugar, and when you serve it in cups you can put a slice of lemon on the outside.

(L.R., Vol. II/216)

81

To Her Nephew Luis Cabrera y Wilson

February 14, 1931

Veni Sancte!

My dear nephew Luis:

I cannot thank you enough for Father Pro's relics (1). It is a shame they are all gone. Ask him to intercede for a need with all your strength, and offer to publicize it for him and whatever else you desire. If he pays attention to you I will advise you. Of course, I will also pray with great faith. I am sending you these relics that they sent to me from León; you will see that they will send us another. See if they are what you wanted. I asked for them from Bishop Valverde (2), and his niece (3) sent them.

Your mother (4) and Angelita (5) are well. There is a terrible epidemic of flu here. They say there are two hundred thousand cases. Here everyone has been ill, Carlos (6), Pancho (7), Ignacio (8), etc.

So become a saint and do not forget me in your prayers. Your aunt who loves you so much.

Concepción

Regards to Luciano (9). I already knew of the young man Lapuente (10); Manuel (11) had written me, and his mother (12) pays me visits.

(L.R., Vol. IV 130-131)

(1) Father Miguel Agustín Pro, S.J., a Mexican martyr whose feast is celebrated on November 23rd in the United States.

(2) His Excellency, Emeterio Valverde y Téllez, Bishop of León. Confessor of Mrs. Armida from September 22, 1904, to May 1905, and again from 1917 to 1925.

(3) Bishop Valverde had two nieces, Guadalupe and Josefina.

(4) Carlota Wilson y Urquidi, widow of her brother Luis Cabrera y Arias.

(5) Angela Cabrera y Wilson, sister of Father Luis and a daughter of Carlota Wilson and Luis Cabrera y Arias. She died on December 15, 1984. Father Luis died on January 26, 1985.

(6) Carlos Lafarga Aragón y Vallejo, husband of Guadalupe Armida y Cabrera.

(7) Francisco Armida y Cabrera.

(8) Ignacio Armida y Cabrera.

(9) Possibly Father Luciano Blanco Morán, S.J., nephew of Isabel Morán, the wife of Ignacio Armida y Cabrera.

(10) A young man who entered the Society of Jesus.

(11) Father Manuel Armida y Cabrera, S.J.

(12) This young man's mother used to visit Mrs. Armida.

82

To Her Niece Carlota Cabrera y Wilson

1 Jardín Centenario
Coyoacán, Mexico City
January 21, 1926
Mother Carlota Cabrera y Wilson
Monterrey

My dear niece:

I greatly appreciated your letter of condolence for the death of my angelical Teresa (1). And to the Mothers (2) and to you, for your prayers; please express my gratitude to them. The Lord took what was His own! Blessed be the Lord! I love His divine will with all my heart, I kiss and adore it, because it is always lovable, even though it crucifies us. Naturally my motherly heart bleeds, but He has helped me, He is so good! Teresa has not died; she now lives the true life, and Jesus has set for me a new attraction to heaven. I only ask Him for one consolation, the one of consoling Him; help me to obtain this.

Teresa suffered body and soul for almost two years. "Our Lord," she said, "is purifying me to take me," and she was so certain of this that she had made a deal with Saint Thérèse (3) (who obtained for her all she desired) to take her to heaven before the year of her canonization was over. "I am going to die," she said during her last communal recreation and wrote the same thing to León (4) and she told me so, and said she was happy so as not to offend God.

A short time earlier the community (5) had their spiritual exercises with Primitivo, and he told me that Teresa had been very fervent in them, so as to prepare for death. If you could only see her spiritual writings, how profound they were and how detached she was from earth. She never thought of herself as being of any value; and her superiors (6) said she was notable for her hidden life, her humility and her charity. I encouraged her (the Archbishop (7) gave me permission to be with her nine days before her death), since she so loved Little Thérèse, to ask her in heaven if she could help her keep on tossing roses to the earth. I did not do anything for her, only saw her, but I did assist her towards a good death several times, and she commended her own soul to the Lord with great fervor. She completely forgot herself during her illness and offered everything for souls. "Heaven, heaven!" she said. "When are You going to take me with You, my Jesus?" Many acts of love and contrition.

The priests (8) took turns day and night and absolved her. "I am at peace," she said, "give me absolution, I have nothing more to say." On the 20th at 9:00, they took her to the chapel and there was a Vigil and solemn Mass by the Missionaries (9) and the funeral was at 3:00, and they also carried her away singing psalms and responses. I went down to the crypt (10) until the bricklayers finished, then I came back home.

So do not forget to pray for the two CONCHAS (11) and ask the good Mothers, whom Teresa so loved, to pray also. Become a saint, which is the only thing necessary.

Your aunt who loves you so embraces you.

Concepción

I hope Teresa settles the matter regarding Julia (12). I love her.

(L.R., Vol. II/101-102)

(1) Concepción Armida y Cabrera entered the Sisters of the Cross of the Sacred Heart of Jesus and received the name of Teresa de María Inmaculada. She was first sent to the House of Puebla and later to the one at Monterrey. She died on December 19, 1925 (see letters 25-36).

(2) The religious of the Society of the Sacred Heart, to which this niece belonged.

(3) Saint Thérèse of the Infant Jesus, to whom she was very devoted. She assumed this name in religious life.

(4) The House of the Sisters of the Cross of the Sacred Heart of Jesus in León, Guanajuato.

(5) The Community of the Sisters of the Cross of the Sacred Heart of Jesus at the Mother House, on Mirto Street, where Sister Teresa lived and died.

(6) The Superiors of Sister Teresa.

(7) The Archbishop of Mexico, José Mora y del Río.

(8) The Missionaries of the Holy Spirit, brother Congregation of the Sisters of the Cross for whom Sister Teresa used to pray often, even before its founding in 1914.

(9) The Missionaries of the Holy Spirit.

(10) The crypt of the Sisters of the Cross of the Sacred Heart of Jesus in the Spanish Cemetery in Mexico City. Later, Mrs. Armida would also be buried there.

(11) Sister Teresa de María, formerly Concepción (Concha), and Mrs. Armida (Concha).

(12) Mother Julia Navarrete Guerrero was born in Oaxaca on July 30, 1881, a daughter of Demetrio, a teacher, and Julia. Father Alberto Mir introduced her to the Congregation of the Sisters of the Cross that was in its beginnings. Mother Julia had an active temperament and was a gifted teacher. In 1903, she left this Congregation with thirteen other nuns and founded the Congregation of the Missionary Daughters of the Most Pure Virgin Mary in Aguascalientes. During these years some difficulties arose because of the schools these religious were opening in Mexico City, and Mrs. Armida was afraid this might be damaging to the Sisters of the Cross. Mother Julia founded numerous schools in Mexico, and missions in the United States. She died on November 21, 1974, with a widespread reputation for sanctity.

83

To Her Nephew Ignacio Muriel y Cabrera

Mexico City, May 4, 1920
Sr. Don Ignacio Muriel (1)
San Luis Potosí

My dear Nacho:

I received your letter just in time in which you informed me of your impending marriage to this young girl (2) so worthy and full of virtues; I congratulate you with all my heart and unite myself to your happiness, and to that of your mother (3), for your father will bless this union from heaven. God really did prepare this treasure that is Lupe for you, so beautiful, so kind, and who loves you so; and you well know my prayers on the 8th will be for you both. Ana (4) and I will celebrate from here. I had not written back to you because I have continued to be quite ill, and now with the sorrow that Nacho and Chabela (5) have lost their first baby. I gave your message to Nacho and he told me he was going to write to you. Regards to your brothers and sisters (6) and to Lupe (7) that I congratulate her for her little girl: Ana said she had a good birth.

Your aunt who loves you embraces you.

Concepción C. de Armida
(L.R., Vol. II/201-202)

---

(1) Ignacio Muriel y Cabrera, born on October 12, 1883, in San Luis Potosí, a grandson of Florencio Cabrera and Manuela Otahegui. His parents were María de Jesús Cabrera y Otahegui and Ignacio Muriel Soberón.

(2) Guadalupe de la Maza y de Icaza, daughter of Joaquín de la Maza and of Luz de Icaza y Cossío.

(3) María de Jesús Cabrera y Otahegui.

(4) Reverend Mother Ana Apolonia Cabrera y Otahegui, Superior General of the Sisters of the Cross of the Sacred Heart of Jesus, and also an aunt of Ignacio Muriel.

(5) Ignacio Armida y Cabrera and Isabel Morán y Bolaños Cacho, his wife. Their first child Ignacio died the day after his birth.

(6) The children of the couple Muriel y Cabrera were: Manuela, Ignacio, José Heriberto, José Manuel, José Luis Jaime, Salvador, José de Jesús, María, and Guadalupe.

(7) Guadalupe Muriel y Cabrera married Nicolás Kretchmar y Muriel who was born in Mexico City on April 25, 1920.

84

To Her Nephew Arturo Marti y De Los Heros And Her Niece Luz Cabrera y Hernández

July 18, 1925

Cruz

My dear nephew and niece Arturo and Luz:

Today I passed the day next to the body of Amelia Gómez del Campo (1) who died yesterday; from there I went to see Panchito (2) who continues to be very ill, and upon arriving at home last night, I found Octaviano's letter (3) in which he gives us the news of your great sorrow (4). I accompany you in your grievance with all my heart and would like to be with you to comfort you, although in these cases it is only the Lord who can give strength and resignation to the will.

That little girl was an angel (5) whom God plucked for His glory while she was still in the bud. I cannot forget her playfulness and her love for Memo (6). She was charming on earth but she will be more so in heaven. I accompany you with all my heart and soul, for those who have passed through that sorrow are able to understand its magnitude. We find ourselves here fearful for Panchito (7); he has had typhoid fever for fifteen to seventeen days and has become so thin. He has had no complications up to now, but the fever is the same, the same every day. Let us see what the Lord wills. Ask for his health if this be God's will.

Alberto is heartbroken (8). Amelia also started out with

typhoid for fifty days and after that phlebitis and meningitis; she went blind and, after seventy-six days of being in bed, she died. Because the funeral will be tomorrow at nine and here, because it is Sunday, the post office is open only half a day, I am writing to you at night.

May the Lord comfort you as I ask him to, and may neither Luz nor the baby be too upset. Tomorrow I am going to see Arturo (9) and Ramón (10) to see if they want to come to lunch with me. Poor things, being so far away, they must suffer all the more.

A great embrace from your aunt who loves you.

Concepción
(L.R., Vol. II/197-199)

(1) Wife of Alberto Gómez del Campo.
(2) Mrs. Armida's grandson, Francisco Armida y Baz.
(3) Octaviano Cabrera y Arias, brother of Concepción.
(4) Because of the death of their little girl.
(5) Carmen Marti y Cabrera, born on March 18, 1920.
(6) Guillermo Marti y Cabrera, who came before the little girl.
(7) Her grandchild Francisco Armida y Baz.
(8) Alberto Gómez del Campo, the widower of Amelia.
(9) Arturo Marti y Cabrera, first son of Luz Cabrera and Arturo Marti.
(10) Ramón Marti y Cabrera, third son of that couple.

To Her In-Laws: Nieces and Nephews,
Armida Family

Her In-Laws: Nieces and Nephews, Armida Family

MANUELA VIADERO Y ARMIDA, daughter of Rosario Armida y García — eldest sister of Francisco Armida y García, husband of Concepción — and of Manuel Viadero. They married in 1887, and had ten daughters: Emilia, Carmen, Josefina, Manuela, María, Amalia, Dolores, Rosario, Felipa, and Margarita. During her second marriage to Leopoldo Viadero, brother of her former husband, she had two sons: Manuel and Leopoldo.

MARIA ARMIDA Y CARTENSEN, daughter of Antonio Armida y García — second of the brothers of Francisco Armida y García — and of Emilia Cartensen.

JOSÉ ARMIDA Y TORRES, son of Ildefonso Armida y García — third brother of Francisco Armida y García — and of Damiana Torres. He was born on August 30, 1896. He married Concepción Velasco Taboada. They had three children: José, María Estela, and Teresa. He died in Mexico City on February 18, 1956.

85

To Her Niece Manuela Viadero y Armida

1 Jardín Centenario
Coyoacán, Mexico City
April 20, 1927
Miss Manuela Viadero
San Luis Potosí

My dearest niece:

You cannot imagine the painful surprise I received last night when Salvador brought me, from the office, notice of Emilia's death (1). I did not even know she was ill, and I thought she was already back in Morelia. Receive my heartfelt condolences and I beg you to extend them from all of us to Lola (2) and Amalia (3). God help me! What did she die from? Please send me the details. I did not know that she was suffering from anything serious.

Poor Emilia! She was still so young! But rather blessed, because she escaped so many things, and what a blessing that she was close to you when she died. It was her hour — and happy are we who have faith so that we do not cry like those who have no hope! We shall see our dear departed ones! And their absence is only fleeting because life is only a bridge to eternity, that is the true life, and I believe that, among other reasons, the Lord takes our dear ones from us so that we may have another attraction to heaven.

Once again, let me know the details. I loved Emilia very dearly and I am praying for her soul. And you all? How have you been? I have been ill on top of the present sufferings that are breaking my heart. I am sending you some triduums (4). Salvador sends his regards; one by one receive my sincere condolences. Good-bye, Melita, and your aunt who loves you so embraces you,

Concepción Cabrera de Armida

Just imagine the other day a room off the garden caught fire, and the firemen had to come; the night before last at 9:30 the ceiling of the front room fell in: a lot of dirt, bricks, and a beam. Nothing showed from the outside. Thank God nobody was in there.

(L.R., Vol. II/219-221)

(1) Emilia Viadero y Armida.
(2) Dolores Viadero y Armida.
(3) Amalia Viadero y Armida (Melita).
(4) Prayers to be said during three successive days.

86

To Her Niece Maria Armida y Cartensen

Mexico City, September 1, 1919
Miss María Armida (y Cartensen)
San Luis

My dear María:

Forgive me for not having answered you before this; I have had a lot of work to do finishing the *Manual of the Holy Spirit* (1) which will soon be printed. I was also waiting for the *Chains of Love* (*Cadenas de Amor*) (2) to arrive so that I could send you one, but they are still in Veracruz; they should be here soon along with *Life of Love* (*Vida de Amor*) (3). Listen, I am thinking of sending you two of each one so you could sell them; I would give you twenty per cent if that's all right? Also, if you want to select others, just let me know. If they are not sold, you could send them back to me and that would be the end of it. So I am going to send you a list with the prices and you can tell me if you want me to send them, which ones, and how many; it is better that you choose for yourself.

Father Félix (4) says that if there is no permission for the Family of the Holy Spirit (5) from the Chancery (Bishop's office), he believes it would be better not to organize choirs [groups of 20 or so] and devotees until everything is in order; those people who want to be inscribed should send a list of their names. Rome will soon grant the indulgences. The same for the Apostleship (6). As a devotee you can arrange with Amalia (7) to lead the members of these choirs until the Missionaries of the Holy Spirit (8) can take them over and give them a big boost. With my regards to your mother (9) and to Techa

(10), your aunt who is anxious to see you, fondly embraces you.

Say hello to Carmen (11) and to the Viaderos (12) and Carmelita (13). Tell Carmen that Pancho (14) did not take Concha (15) to Monterrey; he only went by to see the Sisters (16) who were going to establish a House of the Congregation there. I will say goodbye until another occasion.

Concepción
(L.R., Vol. II/8-10)

(1) Book written by Mrs. Armida.

(2) Book that outlines a plan for the spiritual life based on the spirituality of the Cross.

(3) Another book of Mrs. Armida. She sent them to Spain to be printed.

(4) Father Félix de Jesús Rougier, Founder of the Missionaries of the Holy Spirit.

(5) A confraternity also founded by Father Rougier to spread devotion to the Holy Spirit and ways to practice it.

(6) The Apostleship of the Cross, first of the Works of the Cross, to which everyone can be inscribed: faithful, religious, and priests who desire to live the spirituality of these Works.

(7) Amalia Fernández del Castillo, first president of the Apostleship of the Cross.

(8) The Missionaries of the Holy Spirit, who are in charge of promoting all of the works of the Cross.

(9) Emilia Cartensen, wife of Antonio Armida y García, who was a brother of Francisco Armida y García, the husband of Concepción.

(10) Teresa Armida y Cartensen.

(11) Carmen Armida y García, the youngest sister of Francisco Armida y García. She married Eugenio Ortiz.

(12) The ten daughters of Rosario Armida y García and Manuel Viadero were: Emilia, Carmen, Josefina, Manuela, María, Amalia, Dolores, Rosario, Felipa, and Margarita.

(13) Another one of the nieces or relatives of the Armida family.

(14) Francisco Armida y Cabrera.

(15) Concepción Armida y Cabrera who entered with the Sisters of the Cross of the Sacred Heart of Jesus and received the name of Teresa de María Inmaculada.

(16) The Sisters of this Congregation who opened a convent in the city of Monterrey. Later, Sister Teresa was sent to this House.

87

To Her Nephew José Armida y Torres

May 12, 1934

My dear nephew Pepe:

You cannot imagine the sadness that your letter gave me, but blessed be the Lord who knows whom to put to the test, one who can resist as a Christian. Blessed be God!

I talked to Pancho (1) and he tells me that they had two good months and then back again to where they were for a long time; he was very sorry about your situation and for being unable to improve it. Would it be convenient for you to work as a representative? Even if it would be only for mornings or afternoons? About Conchita (2), do not worry, the Lord will provide. I will send some clothes and I am checking to see if Mrs. Perches (3), who has a clinic, may be able to take her in for a modest fee: she helps her son who is the doctor (4); so don't worry about that. Faith and confidence! Oh, by the way, I had to give away the newspaper the "Palabra" of the 10th and I ask you to fetch one for me to keep it for the Sisters (5); they say you wrote it and that it is very nice.

I am worried that Basols (6) (I do not know how it is spelled) might suspend the paper, since he is now in the Ministry of the Interior.

With my regards to your mother (7), to Conchita, and to María Luisa (8) and a thousand hugs for your better half, I bid you good-bye with an embrace. Your aunt who loves you much.

Concepción
(L.R., Vol. II/89-90)

(1) Francisco Armida y Cabrera.

(2) Concepción Velasco Taboada, wife of José Armida y Torres. She died on October 4, 1960.

(3) The mother of Doctor Perches.

(4) Doctor Perches was the administrator of a Maternity Clinic.

(5) The Sisters of the Cross of the Sacred Heart of Jesus. Two sisters of José entered this Congregation: María Guadalupe and Rosa.

(6) Narciso Bassols, Minister of the Interior. He was supposed to be a communist.

(7) Damiana Torres, wife of Ildefonso Armida y García, the third brother of Francisco. They married on July 24, 1894 and had five children: José; María Luisa, single; Rosa, Sister of the Cross; Enrique, married; and María Guadalupe, Sister of the Cross. José was born in Zacatecas on August 31, 1896. He died in Mexico City on February 18, 1956. He married Concepción Velasco Taboada. They had three children: José, María Estela, and Teresa.

(8) María Luisa Armida y Torres, single and a teacher.

88

June 21, 1934

Dear Pepe:

I am telling your mother (1) that I obtained some groceries for you, but they have gone to your house twice and there was nobody home; so I asked them to send them to your mother's house. I think there should be enough for several months. It is also possible that I may obtain a layette ("Canastilla") (2) for Concha — clothes for the little angel that is coming — so you don't have to spend to have one made. I will let you know if this has been arranged, I believe it has. It will also go to your mother's house. Oh, poor Joaquín Valle (3); we have felt this deeply. Pray for him.

Imagine, they are writing to me from Chihuahua asking me to tell my son Francisco (4), the one who writes in the "Palabra", a few things about mines. I am sending you the copied paragraph.

And so my regards to Concha, (5) hugs to the children (6) and your aunt embraces you.

Concepción
(L.R., Vol. I/91)

---

(1) Damiana Torres, native of Jalapa, Veracruz. She married Ildefonso Armida y García, the third brother of Francisco Armida y García. When she became a widow, she looked forward to living near Mrs. Armida.

(2) A layette for the baby (literally "a little basket"), it is called a Moses in other places.

(3) A friend of Francisco Armida y Cabrera and a shareholder in the business for twenty years. He died suddenly.

(4) Francisco Armida y Cabrera.

(5) Concepción Velasco Taboada, the wife of José Armida y Torres.

(6) At the time, José and María Estela Armida y Velasco.

89

July 6, 1934

My dear nephew Pepe:

You must know that this idea that your financial situation is going to go on thus for ages and ages is no inspiration or anything similar. Do not be silly! What they are sending to you is not from the Conference (1) but from a saintly man who is my friend and donates to many people with discretion and reserve. I think he will be sending something to you for a few months. The little bed and its furnishings is quite complete and very pretty; they will send it to your mother's house by the end of September; they do not know for whom it is; this lady makes them to give them away.

So, chin up, do not worry and let us receive things as the Lord wills to send them, everything passes away except having lovingly suffered for God. Yes, the priest arrived on time to Joaquín Valle (2), but though he could no longer speak, he seemed to recognize him.

I do not care one bit about receiving or wearing things given to me. Once — what a laugh — I was wearing eleven things from different persons! So if you are like me in this lack of concern, I have here a suit that Primitivo gave me for whomever I desired to give it. It consists of two pair of trousers, a vest, and a jacket. If you want it, I can send it to your mother's house. If you do not reply, this will mean you do not want it.

A thousand things to Conchita (3), hugs to your babies, regards to your mother, and to María Luisa (4), and Enrique and his wife (5).

Your aunt embraces you.

Concepción
(L.R., Vol. I/ 92-93)

(1) Saint Vincent de Paul Society, a charitable organization known for its apostolate with the poor.

(2) Friend and partner of the business concern of Armida y Cabrera (see letter 88).

(3) Concepción Velasco Taboada, the wife of José Armida y Torres.

(4) María Luisa Armida y Torres, Pepe's sister.

(5) Enrique Armida y Torres, Pepe's brother, and his wife.

90

Morelia, September 18, 1934
Mr. José Armida
Mexico City

My dear nephew, Pepe:

My congratulations for your Teresita (1) who will surely be as precious as her little brother and sister. I also congratulate Damianita (2), Concha (3) and you, and I thank the Lord that, as Lupe (4) tells me, they are all well. I am leaving on Thursday and as soon as I am able to, I will have the pleasure of embracing you. My loving regards and kisses, especially for the new baby. Your aunt who loves you, embraces you.

Concepción
(L.R., Vol. I/94)

(1) Teresa Armida y Velasco, Pepe's little daughter.
(2) Damiana Torres de Armida, Pepe's mother.
(3) Concepción Velasco Taboada de Armida, Pepe's wife.
(4) Guadalupe Armida y Torres, Sister of the Cross of the Sacred Heart of Jesus, Pepe's sister.

To Know the Spirituality of the Cross

Before the Altar: A hundred visits to Jesus in the Blessed Sacrament, Concepción Cabrera de Armida, Marian Press, 2001.

I Am: Eucharistic Meditations on the Gospel, Concepción Cabrera de Armida, Alba House, 2001.

Irresistibly Drawn to the Eucharist: Conchita Cabrera de Armida's Most Beautiful Writings on the Eucharist, Fr. Juan Gutiérrez González, M.Sp.S., Alba House, 2002.

Conchita: A Mother's Spiritual Diary, M.M. Philipon, O.P., Alba House, 1978.

A Modern Mystic, M.M. Philipon, O.P., Acme Printing, Modesto, 2001.

To my Priests, Concepción Cabrera de Armida, published by Archanchel Crusade of Love, Cleveland, 1996.

Our Lady of Solitude, M.M. Philipon, O.P., Libreria Editrice Vaticana, 2001.

You Belong to the Church, Concepción Cabrera de Armida, Pilgrimage to Rome 1913, Libreria Editrice Vaticana, 2000 (in English, Spanish and Italian).

Books in Spanish

Respuesta a la Invasión de Dios, I-II, Juan Gutiérrez, Litográfica, Mexico City, 1994.

Una Mística en el Interior de la Iglesia Madre, Juan Gutiérrez, Encuentro Ediciones, Madrid, 1984.

Concepción Cabrera de Armida I-II-III, Jesús Ma. Padilla, Editorial La Cruz, Mexico City.

Verdad Central, Luis Ruiz Vázquez, Ediciones Cimiento, Mexico City, 1994.

Gracias Para Agradecer, Admirar y Amar, 1925

Amar Con El Espíritu Santo, 1926

Ser Madre, 1927

Ser Jesús Crucificado, 1928

El Interior Del Corazón De Jesús, 1929

Consumación En La Unidad De La Trinidad, 1930

Tercer Amor, 1931-1932

Los Descansos De Jesús, 1933

Dar a Jesús Para Ser Crucificado, 1934

La Encarnación Mística, 1935

La Perfecta Alegría, 1936

Concepción Cabrera de Armida Ejercicios Espirituales, Ediciones Cimiento (Ejercicios guiados por el Arzobispo Luis Ma. Martínez).

Cómo es Jesús, Concepción Cabrera de Armida, Colección TERCER MILENIO, Ediciones Cimiento, Mexico City, 1997.

Abiertos al Espíritu, Concepción Cabrera de Armida, Colección TERCER MILENIO, Ediciones Cimiento, Mexico City, 1998.

¡Mi Padre Dios, Padre Nuestro!, Concepción Cabrera de Armida, Colección TERCER MILENIO, Ediciones Cimiento, Mexico City, 1999.

Jesus, Savior of Mankind, Save Them, Save Them!

For Further Information:

Sisters of the Cross of the Sacred Heart of Jesus
1320 Maze Blvd.
Modesto, CA 95351
Tel/Fax: 1-209-526-3525
E-mail: rcscjmodesto@hotmail.com

Sisters of the Cross of the Sacred Heart of Jesus
Religiose della Croce del Sacro Cuore di Gesù
Via Appia Nuova 1468
00178 Roma, Italia
Tel/ Fax: 06-7-934-0094
E-mail: rel croce@pcn.net

Religiosas de la Cruz del Sagrado Corazón de Jesús
Francisco Sosa, 105
Col. Coyoacán
04000 Mexico, D.F.
Tel: 554-0011; Fax: 554-0335
E-mail: cimientocoyo@hotmail.com

Missionaries of the Holy Spirit
Christ the Priest Province
P.O. Box 956
Garden Grove, CA 92842-0956
USA
Tel: (714) 534-5476
Fax: (714) 534-5184

Missionari dello Spirito Santo
Piazza San Salvatore in Campo 57
00186 Rome, Italy
Tel: 06-68-10-1301; Fax: 686-8760
E-mail: mspsroma@iname.com